Tao *of* Founders

Creative Director: Saeah Wood
Production and Editorial Manager: Amy Reed
Editorial: Amy Reed, Matthew Hoover, and Christa Evans
Design: Ivica Jandrijević

Library of Congress Control Number: 2024920043

Paperback ISBN: 978-1-955671-46-0
E-book ISBN: 978-1-955671-47-7
Audiobook ISBN: 978-1-955671-48-4

ensemble.ventures
taooffounders.com

otterpine.com
Asheville, North Carolina

Tao *of* Founders

◆ ◆ ◆

Timeless Insights for
Resilient Entrepreneurs

Guillaume Racine

To Théodore, Lisa, and Cécile

CONTENTS

Duality and Your Hero's Journey

Do you know the best thing about startups?...You only ever experience two emotions: euphoria and terror.
—BEN HOROWITZ

Entrepreneurship can be extreme. Bouncing from wild emotion to wild emotion, it can feel difficult to find inner peace. Living exposed to the extremes can contribute to a sense of burnout that is, unfortunately, quite common for entrepreneurs. As a founder, I've often wondered how I can find my emotional footing, a sense of balance amid a busy and chaotic way of life.

One day I came across the Tao Te Ching. Written in China around 400 BC, the book is short and timeless. With a deceptively simple format, the Tao Te Ching is in fact pretty deep; it explores ideas that are just as relevant for us today as they were for people two and a half millennia ago.

What is Tao?

The concept of "Tao," which is the foundation for the Taoist tradition, translates to "the way" or "the path." The Tao can be interpreted in many ways. One interpretation is the Tao as the natural order of the universe. Taoism teaches that extreme thinking runs counter to the natural harmony of the universe. By following the natural flow of things—nurturing equanimity, and taking effortless action with deep intentions, you can live with a greater sense of harmony between your inner reality and the world you exist in.

To me, the Tao holds a solution to the extremes of entrepreneurial life. It points the way to a grounded and resilient mindset. The Tao Te Ching is old: over two thousand years ago, humans were struggling with the same inner conflicts as we do today. The search for inner peace and balance is a timeless, universal theme.

I wrote *Tao of Founders* inspired by the ideas within the Tao Te Ching, and with a clear audience in mind: entrepreneurs. This book is about mindset more than occupation. To me, being an entrepreneur is a mindset, a creative way of being. Founders are not defined by their job title. Not everyone is an entrepreneur, but everyone can be entrepreneurial. I wrote this book for those who want to better understand and approach the inner aspects of entrepreneurship, for those seeking resilience, all while navigating a generally chaotic and challenging life.

Duality and the founder journey

The hero's journey is a universal storytelling framework used in books, movies, etc. that describes the transformative adventure of a hero who leaves their ordinary world, faces and overcomes significant challenges, and returns home changed, often with newfound wisdom or a valuable boon. This structure highlights the hero's growth and resilience, and the essential interplay between departure, initiation, and return, making it a powerful tool for storytelling across cultures and genres.

As a founder, you are writing your own version of the classic hero's journey: You face a series of challenges that show up in various ways through the physical (outer) and the emotional (inner) aspects of your lived reality. The founder journey resembles the arc of the hero's journey, as outlined below.

HERO'S JOURNEY	FOUNDER JOURNEY
Call to Adventure	Inspiration to solve a problem, create a product, or disrupt an industry
Refusal of the Call	Doubts and fears about abilities, risks, and potential failure
Meeting the Mentor	Seeking mentors, advisors, or experienced entrepreneurs for guidance
Crossing the Threshold	Stepping into the world of entrepreneurship, leaving behind security
Tests, Allies, and Enemies	Facing challenges, building a team, securing funding, and navigating competition
Approach to the Inmost Cave	Critical phases that threaten survival and success: new product launches, new market entry, or closing on partnerships
Ordeal	Significant hurdles such as financial crises, product failures, or major pivots
Reward (Seizing the Sword)	Achieving product-market fit, gaining traction, or securing major investments
The Road Back	Scaling the business, refining operations, and facing new challenges as they grow
Resurrection	Meeting critical turning points like acquisition offers, IPOs, or strategic decisions
Return with the Elixir	Sharing knowledge, mentoring new entrepreneurs, and contributing to the entrepreneurial ecosystem

As you progress on your journey, your external problems and your emotional landscape may appear unrelated to each other, like black and white, but in fact they arise together. In Buddhist terms, the object (your reality) and the subject (your mind) are said to "co-arise," since nothing exists independently.[*]

There are no fixed separations between your inner and outer worlds. Labeling your issues as only inside or outside challenges introduces a dualistic perspective. The thing is, duality is a human invention. All things you label as a problem arise only from one place: your mind. Taoist traditions understand the non-dualistic nature of life and reality. Embracing a non-dualistic view means that you don't need to choose between A and B, even when they appear opposed, like the yin and the yang. Yin and yang form a whole, a circle. In the same vein, a sense of balance, or inner peace, is sometimes easier to achieve when opposites are paired together, by embracing contradictions.

---

[*] Though Buddhism and Taoism are distinct spiritual traditions, there is much crossover. I have been inspired by the wisdom of many Eastern traditions, so I will be referencing a few throughout this book.

A non-dual mindset might help you feel less exposed by moving away from the extremes, by not believing in them. Working on being more centered brings you clarity, consistency, and momentum. These qualities will guide you as you advance on your own founder journey.

Why talk about duality in entrepreneurship?

Entrepreneurship is full of paradoxes: They will test the founder at various stages of their journey. By handling the paradoxes well, founders gain the opportunity to move closer to their potential. Paradoxes make you believe your reality is black or white when in fact it is black *and* white—and all the hues of gray in between. The thing is that a paradox, by definition, cannot be solved. So quit trying. The only real way to solve a paradox is through seeking a different frame of mind and being comfortable with ambiguity—moving past duality.

We'll look into many entrepreneurial paradoxes throughout this book. Each chapter in *Tao of Founders* is an exploration of distinct and timeless insights that can help you embrace some of the most common paradoxes you encounter as a founder. For example:

- You hold unwavering faith in ultimate success, while confronting the brutal and humbling facts of your current reality.

- You rely on the help of others to reach your dreams, while trying to not care too deeply about what they think of you.

- You are a human being, not a human doing—and your identity is not your startup.

Your founder journey is about overcoming yourself

At the core of every hero's journey, the hero's inner realm evolves directly in relation to the external problems that call them to push through their limits. The hero overcomes problems by *overcoming themselves*. By focusing inward, the hero is equipped to better handle reality and all its challenges. I believe that the most common (and least discussed) obstacles for startup growth are the founder's emotional ability to see clearly and face what is needed of them.

By learning to better approach your problems from an inner perspective, you equip yourself with better tools to tackle all of your challenges, and by extension, to help your employees and colleagues tackle their own problems. It all starts within. Your challenges and your difficult emotions are road signs showing you the way to a better version of yourself—if you lean into them.

Why I wrote this book

As I said, when I first became a founder, my emotions felt extreme for the entire ride, from start to exit. I often couldn't tell how I felt because I felt euphoria and terror *at the same time.*

The emotional roller coaster did not stop when we sold our startup. When the company I co-founded, Return Magic, was acquired by Shopify, I had to navigate a new set of emotional and motivational challenges. Now an employee, I lost some of the independence I valued. I had to redefine my purpose, my work identity. I really wanted to be accepted and respected by a bunch of brilliant colleagues, and I wanted to prove that we were worth acquiring in the first place—that we were worth taking a bet on. Proving my worth and fueling my ego caused me to build emotional debt; I repressed emotions that I was unwilling or unable to fully experience. Instead of dealing with my emotions to let them go, I built up invisible weight on myself that pulled my mind down. I didn't have enough time or energy to really care deeply about anything. I felt like a dimmed version of myself. A lifetime of unmanaged thoughts and emotions had built up, and all of it was boiling over now.

On the outside, it appeared like I had found success. I was ticking some of those traditional "success" boxes, yet I felt mostly numb. Chronic stress turned to depression. I didn't want others to see me struggle, which led me to hide my emotions even deeper.

About six months after my company was acquired, bearing the weight of my fossilized identity, I kept wondering why I felt bad all the time. Fortunately, with the help of an executive coach and therapist, I worked on reframing how I view and talk to myself. These coaching sessions were the start of a series of insights that would culminate with the book you are reading right now. I hadn't planned to share these personal lessons, but I felt compelled to offer my fellow founders a few insights I learned the hard way.

The reason I bring up some of my issues here is because all founders experience their own flavor of struggle, whether it shows or not, whether they admit it or not, and whether they know it or not. As a founder, you're playing life on hard mode, but that doesn't mean you should struggle alone. Sharing openly invites others to do the same.

Chances are the big problem you have today is nothing new. Other founders have likely experienced it and have already found effective ways to overcome similar challenges. You are not alone. Exposing what makes you vulnerable may feel uncomfortable, but sharing your challenges is what enables other founders to relate to you. It's a small price to pay for the potentially life-changing upside that comes from tapping into collective wisdom.

When things feel especially hard, it helps me to remember it's not all on my shoulders. I can always lean on the wisdom of those who have come before me, or seek the advice of a peer. Somehow, all of our individual hero journeys are intertwined.

The reward a founder gets for solving problems is bigger problems to solve. Sooner or later some problems will feel overwhelming to you. I hope this book serves as your emotional survival kit when you experience the challenging feelings that are part of the entrepreneurial course.

Now let's get to it.

We are human beings, not human doings. —ADRIAN HOWELL

Cultivate Agency

*Freedom is the will to be
responsible for ourselves.*
—FRIEDRICH NIETZSCHE

The essence of struggling and suffering lies in your *framing*. Let's imagine you're running a marathon. In one scenario, you're told to run at gunpoint. In another one, you're running while being cheered on by friends and family. The amount of energy you burn is the same. But the feeling you get when running is not. Why?

Your perception of having a *choice*—or lack there-of—defines how you feel in a situation. Feeling a sense of choosing your struggles makes them empowering, while feeling powerless makes everything harder. Having a choice is less about the objective truth and more about what you choose to believe.

Your frame of mind, therefore, is the major defining factor of your lived experience. Framing with *high agency* is to nurture a sense of fully choosing your challenges—regardless of whether you actually did so. When choice seems illusory, you can reframe by thinking about how you'd act if you'd fully chosen the situation you're facing. Speaking for myself, I've noticed that assuming agency opens a brighter and more empowering perspective. It takes me out of feeling stuck, doomed, or forced into something, and moves me into a proactive mindset.

The story of the *Endurance*, one of the early expeditions to the South Pole, is a prime example of cultivating agency.[*] In 1914, Ernest Shackleton embarked on an entrepreneurial adventure, a voyage to the unknown, a one-way ticket to the impossible. After *Endurance* eventually sunk, leaving the men

[*] To read the whole story of Shackleton and his crew's harrowing journey, I recommend *Endurance: Shackleton's Incredible Voyage* by Alfred Lansing, originally published in 1959.

stranded on ice, Shackleton's ability to maintain his crew's morale under extreme conditions, navigate leadership challenges, and make critical decisions for survival showcases a stellar attitude in a dire situation. His leadership influenced his men to choose agency as well, despite having no way to coordinate rescue. After living on ice for almost two years, all 28 members of the expedition miraculously survived. Their survival is largely attributed to the character of Shackleton and his men: They remained resilient, choosing to believe they could get out of their "hopeless" situation. Without high agency, I doubt these men would have fought long enough to survive.

Every human faces unchosen events. That's the very nature of life—and the nature of entrepreneurship. But when you consider where your challenges come from, you'll find that many are self-generated. You may think you did not choose them when, in fact, you simply didn't see them coming. You may not be to blame. But how you relate to the challenge is always your responsibility—especially in situations you regard as unfair.

Polaroid vs. Kodak: A modern spin on David and Goliath

In the 1940s, Polaroid's instant photography technology was a revolutionary development, enabling picture-takers to develop prints on their own, in a matter of seconds. Instant photography was a huge commercial hit. In the 1950s and 1960s, Polaroid was essentially the Apple of the post-WWII era; the public revered their inventive, user-centric products.

In the 1970s, drawn to the success of Polaroid, Kodak entered the instant photo market. Then over 10 times the size of Polaroid, Kodak apparently stole Polaroid's intellectual property in order to destroy them. In no time, Polaroid went from being the undisputed market leader to scrambling for survival. They filed a lawsuit, stating Kodak's products directly infringed on their patents and proprietary technology. Clearly, Polaroid was under existential threat and the odds seemed overwhelmingly against them.

Following a legal battle that lasted 10 years, Kodak was found guilty of infringing on Polaroid's patents and was ordered to cease the production of its instant cameras and film, with a $1 billion fine for past actions—easily one of the largest patent settlements at the time. Polaroid had fought for their survival for 10 long years and prevailed against the odds.

The founder of Polaroid, Edwin Land, understood that when you create something groundbreaking, others will inevitably try to copy it. It's just the price of success. Land's response to Kodak's actions was composed, assertive, and strategic. He was determined to protect Polaroid's innovations and market share. He kept his mind actively working on his options, choosing to build instead of fueling the drama.

What Edwin Land did not do was become angry or blame others. His knew his success was his own responsibility, so he used his energies on finding a solution instead of trapping himself emotionally in blame and self-pity. He refused to be a victim to Kodak.

Land understood he had to deal with the consequences that came with his specific choice of work and the inevitable competition. He showed agency in the face of potential ruin. He chose to carry his best self as if he had opted in to the situation.

THE TALE OF THE POISONED ARROW

A man was shot with a poisoned arrow. Instead of removing the arrow, he demanded to know the identity of the shooter, the kind of bow used, and the type of poison on the arrow. He died as a result of focusing his attention on the background instead of the immediate problem—his wound.

This old Buddhist tale illustrates the fallacy of the victim mindset. It serves as a metaphor for how people often focus on the context (why, who, what) of a situation instead of addressing the real source of suffering.

As a founder, thinking of yourself as a victim is risky. This is where you have a choice: Are you a victim or a survivor?* A survivor narrative is high agency in action.

Your painful emotions are useful. Feeling and overcoming pain leads to resilience and inner strength.

---

* A great (and short) explanation of victim vs. survivor mindset can be found in the article "Create and Curate" on the Farnam Street Brain Food blog: https://fs.blog/brain-food/july-2-2023/.

Experiencing pain can increase your empathy and compassion for other people who are suffering. It can clarify what truly matters to you, helping you prioritize your goals and aspirations. Pain often prompts individuals to reflect on deeper existential questions about the meaning of life, suffering, and their place in the world. It can be a powerful source of inspiration for artistic and creative endeavors. All this to say: In short, pain produces meaning. Meaning produces motivation. Motivation produces action. Frame your pain with agency.

> *Two little mice fell in a bucket of cream. The first mouse quickly gave up and drowned. The second mouse wouldn't quit. He struggled so hard that eventually he churned that cream into butter and crawled out.*
> —FRANK ABAGNALE SR. (PLAYED BY CHRISTOPHER WALKEN), *CATCH ME IF YOU CAN*

Judge Kindly

The more one judges, the less one loves. —HONORÉ DE BALZAC

Founders roll through dozens of decisions each day. Your role demands that you spend hours evaluating, comparing, and deciding what is best for you and your startup. The quality of those decisions ultimately determines the quality of your work.

Decisions require you to judge and to establish preferences. You apply a form of judgment on everything you do: hiring, building products, writing emails, communicating priorities with your team, and so on.

Good decisions are about making good trade-offs: what to keep, what to discard, what's important, what to ignore. Good decisions command you to define mental shortcuts, also known as heuristics, that will help you move forward without too much effort.

Good decisions and good trade-offs boil down to focus. You don't need to have the full picture if you can focus on the most important things. In fact, you'll likely never have the full picture before making a decision. Jeff Bezos looks for 70 percent certainty in order to make most decisions. That is the trade-off Amazon is willing to make with most decisions, embracing speed and learning over completeness.

Good decisions usually demand you reach a conclusion based on your imperfect information, imperfect judgment, and imperfect timing. Dealing with a constant stream of decisions each day, small and large, made with incomplete information, invites a new habit to form in your mind: You tend to jump to conclusions. Jumping ahead is good from a decision speed and agility viewpoint. However, jumping to conclusions as a habit can encourage you to judge readily, sometimes harshly.

I've definitely noticed that pattern getting stronger in my mind as my founder journey goes on. With each decision piling up through the years, I feel, well, judgier. By trying to decide faster, I sometimes forget to suspend my own preconceptions. Past a certain point,

I stop listening with the intent to understand; rather, I listen to confirm my decision. I haven't always listened as well as I should have. Listening closely to customers, employees, and partners is probably the lifeline of entrepreneurs, a prerequisite to doing anything of value. Judging harshly makes it so much harder to see the finer nuances of reality as it is. It took me a while to learn how judgment creates separation.

Many of us are quick to judge, yet we don't want to be judged by others. Imagine the last time someone judged you mistakenly because they had imperfect information. Maybe they jumped to conclusions or failed to give you the benefit of the doubt. How did that make you feel? No one enjoys feeling judged unfairly. Harsh judgment can be very damaging to relationships. The moment someone feels judged harshly by someone else, two things will likely happen. Either the person being judged agrees with the judgment and feels shame, or they disagree with the judgment and feel anger. There are no scenarios I can think of where harsh judgment leads to a positive interaction.

As therapist, author, and Buddhist teacher Tara Brach explains, "Judgment is when we're making others bad. The deal is, as far as I can tell, we get accustomed to it. We get accustomed to demoting people in our minds and in our hearts. We get accustomed to the distance it creates."*

For a founder, judging people from a place of "bad others" can be devastating to your team. Constant judging will soon turn to blame. It will be felt and heard by your colleagues and your loved ones. Feeling judged, or avoiding being judged, shuts people down. Judgment prevents them from doing their best work because they fear blame and shame.

In a notable anecdote in *Creativity, Inc.: Overcoming the Unseen Forces That Stand in the Way of True Inspiration*, Ed Catmull, co-founder of Pixar and former president of Walt Disney Animation Studios, addresses how the fear of judgment hinders creativity. Catmull explains that during Pixar's "Braintrust" sessions, they discovered that employees hesitated to share ideas because they feared negative judgment. So Pixar shifted the focus from critiquing the person who proposed an

---

* See Tara Brach's lecture on Disarming Our Hearts: www.youtube .com/watch?v=iGO3XwxXM-k.

idea to evaluating the idea itself.* This subtle change in approach fostered a more open and creative environment, where team members could freely share and explore unproven ideas without fear. If you want your team to feel safe and creative, hold back on judgment, especially when coming from a place of *bad others*. Debate the ideas, not the people.

The weight of harsh judgment

> *People hasten to judge in order not to be judged themselves.*
> —ALBERT CAMUS

Over time, harsh judgment builds into an emotional burden. This negative energy dampens your spirit. In a way, judgment accidentally trains the mind to be rigid. You believe you know how things should be, which is a

---

* Watch Ed Catmull explain the Braintrust concept: www.youtube .com/watch?v=I1Mr3oKR7cM.

stubborn view of the world. The more you believe you know, the harder you become to satisfy. Others just don't know what you know, they don't understand, they don't have the same eye for detail, etc. Those *bad others*. With this mindset, you think no one else can match your standard of quality, your level of dedication. In other words, you become intolerant. You end up trying to control the world around you, asking others to conform to what you judge as acceptable. Living like this is exhausting.

Harsh judgment can also hinder your mission

Harsh judgment did hinder founder Yvon Chouinard in the early days of Patagonia. His attitude toward others made it hard for him to bring the best out of his team. Originally, Chouinard started the company as a way to fuel his passion for the outdoors and the environment. He never saw himself as a businessman. From the start, the young and brash Chouinard was dedicated to quality and environmental sustainability. He was unwavering, and he held himself and others to very high standards. He often found himself frustrated with employees who didn't share his level of passion for environmental issues. He judged those around him who were more focused on the business's financial aspects or who didn't immediately grasp the importance of sustainable practices. This kind of good/bad judgment created a divide within his company, leading to internal conflicts and a lack of cohesion. Chouinard's attitude directly led to frustration among employees, who felt their efforts were not appreciated or understood. Turnover was high.

Over time, Chouinard became wiser. He came to understand the value of balancing business and sustainability goals to achieve the biggest impact. He became more tolerant of employees with different views. While he discerned the different perspectives, he did not get caught up emotionally in blame. Chouinard learned that leading by example and educating his team about the importance of their mission could bring them on board much more effectively. He focused on fostering a shared sense of purpose rather than judging others for not initially seeing things his way. His new approach cultivated a deep sense of community and collective responsibility within Patagonia. Nowadays Patagonia aims to inspire and implement solutions to the environmental crisis through its business practices.

Indeed, Patagonia and Chouinard are known for being very vocal about the urgency of reversing climate change to save all life on earth; the company has remained true to its authentic spirit. At the same time, Patagonia understands that humans are part of both environmental problems and solutions; blaming others and "bad othering" might actually be counterproductive to solving the climate issue. Advocacy and community are the solution. This activist yet inclusive approach to their mission is what makes Patagonia such a special company. I like to believe that Chouinard's personal growth toward wiser discernment, as opposed to harsh judgment, is a secret ingredient that explains why the brand is so globally beloved and relevant today—by the general public, not just climate activists.

Harsh judgment makes you lonely

Bad othering leads you to a duality-based reality, where you see yourself pitted against others; it's you alone against the world. That mental separation takes away the fondness and the empathy that give you connection. Soon, you stop trying to connect to others, and you start wondering why you feel lonely.

> *When you judge another, you do not define them, you define yourself.*
> —WAYNE DYER

Harsh judgment turned inward impairs your self-esteem by emphasizing your flaws over your strengths, and justifying the blame you put on yourself. Self-blame pushes you to find relief or validation outside your own self. You go around looking for proof of your worth. You end up with unrealistic expectations of perfection, and you avoid taking on challenges because you fear feeling inferior and inadequate. You end up even more disconnected from other people and out of touch with yourself.

Moving from harsh judgment to wise discernment

To be clear, I don't think we can avoid judging entirely—but there is a better way to do it. A habit of blaming is a signal for change. It is a call to moderate, reframe, or eliminate judgment that comes from a place of separation. Not jumping to harsh judgment frees you up emotionally, making room for a brighter narrative to fill your mind.

By removing harsh judgment, you free yourself to adopt a habit of wise discernment. Wise discernment is noticing a situation without the emotional turmoil that harsh judgment brings. It starts by seeing the good in others. Using wise discernment, you can see what is happening without feeling that separation. Discernment allows you to still feel that connection, that sense of unity with others. It leaves room for empathy, compassion, and open-mindedness. In contrast, harsh judgment does not value others' views and feelings.

Ultimately, wise discernment feels brighter and more optimistic. It will take you further and help you feel more serene. Discernment doesn't urge you to re-arrange and control the world around you; it lets you see clearly that you are the "other" too.

THE TALE OF TWO MONKS

Two monks, one old and one young, embarked on a pilgrimage. Along their journey, they encountered a young woman unable to cross the muddy banks of the river. Without hesitation, the old monk lifted her and carried her across. The young monk judged in silence, perturbed by this breach of monastic rules that forbid physical contact with a woman. After miles of walking, he finally voiced his disapproval. The old monk smiled gently and said, "I left the woman by the river's edge. Yet you still carry her in your mind."

This Zen Buddhist story highlights the charge and weight that harsh judgment holds, and how it can keep us from being our best selves. Judge kindly.

We can never judge the lives of others, because each person knows only their own pain and renunciation. It's one thing to feel that you are on the right path, but it's another to think that yours is the only path. —PAULO COELHO

Be Water, My Friend

In the beginner's mind there are many possibilities, but in the expert's mind, there are few.
— SHUNRYU SUZUKI

Bruce Lee was known as a martial artist and an actor. He was also a deep thinker, a philosopher. Bruce Lee's real journey was about the mastery of the *self*. His craft, martial arts and movies, happened to be the creative expression of his core principles for life.

Lee famously said, "Be water, my friend."* He was careful to not become too attached to any specific

---

* Watch this great short video of Bruce Lee explaining the metaphor of being like water: www.youtube.com/watch?v=cJMwBwFj5nQ.

idea, remaining mentally fluid. Lee perfected the art of unlearning and undoing his conditioning as the path to authentic self-expression. He was aware that collecting knowledge and habits throughout life can be a burden. Lee understood he was at risk of living on autopilot, blinded by his conditioned behavior, and he recognized that knowledge and training have the ability to get in the way of mastery. This is a paradox of true mastery: Learn your craft deeply, then forget everything. Unlearning is harder because you're working against your conditioning. Learning is a lot more intuitive than unlearning.

> *Obey the principles without being bound by them.* —BRUCE LEE

Unlearning means you need to unsee things—this is a big challenge. Unseeing is counterintuitive because humans are excellent at seeing patterns everywhere, even where none exist. There are countless examples of false patterns humans believe in, despite contrary evidence. For instance, *pareidolia* is the tendency to see images or meaningful patterns in random stimuli, like clouds or burnt toast. The *hot hand fallacy* is the belief that a basketball player has a higher chance of making a shot after a streak of successful shots, despite statistical evidence showing it's a misconception. The *Bible code* refers to alleged hidden messages found in the Bible through equidistant letter sequences (which has been shown to appear in any large text, given enough effort).

In the arena of entrepreneurship, false patterns can take many forms. *Survivorship bias* is focusing on successful startups and ignoring those that failed, leading to false conclusions about what makes startups successful. *First-mover advantage* is believing that being first to market is crucial to success, overlooking the many first movers who failed. The *myth of the lone genius* is believing that successful startups are founded by single geniuses, such as Elon Musk or Steve Jobs, when in fact most, if not all, have achieved greatness due to strong teams that are ultimately the ones turning the company's mission into action.

Fast-and-loose pattern recognition is less useful today than it was in our cave days. The modern world has become much more complex; the skills needed to thrive as a human have evolved. Knowing less can actually help you make better decisions. Less information means you're less likely to see false patterns and better able to discern which pieces of data are actually relevant and valuable.

Your ability to unsee patterns and experience a situation as if for the first time brings us to the concept of *beginner's mind*, known as shoshin in the Zen Buddhist tradition. Shoshin refers to having an attitude of openness, eagerness, and lack of preconceptions when learning, even at an advanced level—just as a beginner would. Shoshin trains the mind to experience things as if for the first time. This subtle shift in mindset is surprisingly powerful. A beginner's mindset is a great mindset to embrace as a founder because it is one full of possibilities and enthusiasm.

Wu wei, the lost art of effortless action

Another subtle yet powerful change in perspective that can help founders be more fluid in their approach is to embrace wu wei, a Taoist concept that roughly means *effortless action*. Wu wei proposes that you let things happen naturally on their own, without trying so hard to control them. Instead of straining, save your effort for the right time to take deliberate, intentional action.

A perfect example: Chameleons can spend over 90 percent of their lives completely motionless, while eating a daily average of 10 flies. They hunt with minimal movement, saving their effort for when the conditions are right. They don't go chasing after flies, they don't read books on how to catch more flies, and they don't set ambitious fly-catching goals. Instead, they do nothing, waiting patiently until a fly comes by. They strike at the best possible moment, all at once. Chameleons are effective because of all the things they *don't* do.

Wu wei does not mean being lazy or passive. It means being at peace and preserving yourself for when effort matters most. It suggests that the most effective form of action is one that does not involve struggle or excessive effort. That's another way of being water: Rivers flow around obstacles, using the path of least resistance, not trying to force anything other than the natural course of things. Wu wei takes into account the natural ebbs and flows of the world.

Survival requires adaptation, greatness requires reinvention

The ability to continually reinvent is what separates the merely good from great founders, artists, and creators. Adaptation is a great skill and a given for survival, but it doesn't guarantee you authentic greatness like reinvention does. Reinvention comes from the application of timeless principles like shoshin and wu wei so that you can remain open, present, ready, and willing to make the changes that your current challenges demand of you.

I've noticed that true masters in all creative fields seem to enjoy the process of reinvention in and of itself. Especially the uncomfortable parts others tend to avoid. The best have the courage to let go of what worked for them in the past, and they try to start again and again, only each time bolder and better. I can't prove it, but I believe that being eager to begin again, endlessly, is what the greatest have in common. They embrace past experiences, while keeping their door open to what's next, to find new ways. Letting go of what has worked for us is often the hardest part for everyone. As Bruce Lee said: "The creative process is a process of surrender, not control."

Just take a look at the following list of creative icons and the huge leaps of reinvention that made them best-in-class in their respective fields.

THE REINVENTION OF ICONS

NAME	FIELD	EARLY WORK	LATER WORK
The Beatles	Music	"Please Please Me" (early pop rock hits)	*Abbey Road, Let It Be* (experimental, mature albums)
Arnold Schwarzenegger	Bodybuilding, acting, politics	Mr. Universe, *The Terminator* (action film)	Governor of California
Serena Williams	Tennis, business	Early Grand Slam wins	Fashion design and business ventures
Benjamin Franklin	Science, politics, publishing	Inventions (lightning rod, bifocals)	Founding Father of the United States
Jim Clark	Technology	University professor	Netscape, WebMD, Shutterfly, SGI
Stephen King	Writing	*Carrie* (horror novel)	*11/22/63* (historical fiction)
Pablo Picasso	Painting	Blue Period (somber paintings in shades of blue)	Cubism (abstract, fragmented forms)
Jeff Bezos	Technology	Quantitative investor on Wall Street	Amazon, Blue Origin

TRANSITION(S)	WHAT MAKES THEM SPECIAL?
Evolved from pop rock to pioneering experimental and studio techniques, influencing global music culture.	Each Beatles album created a new sub-genre—they evolved by keeping a core musical identity, achieving unparalleled commercial success and cultural significance.
Transitioned from a successful career in bodybuilding and acting to a prominent political role as the governor of California.	His unique career path from entertainment to politics, showcasing his diverse talents and ability to impact different fields.
Expanded her career from tennis dominance to entrepreneurship, launching her own fashion line and business ventures.	Her ability to dominate in sports while successfully branching out into fashion and business, showcasing multifaceted talent.
Transitioned from scientific and practical inventions to playing a crucial role in the founding of the United States and its early political framework.	His diverse contributions to science, politics, and society, making lasting impacts in multiple fields.
Moved from a professor role at Stanford to found Silicon Graphics in his late thirties.	Prolific founder behind many technology businesses across diverse industries. Invented the first widely used web browser.
Expanded his storytelling from pure horror to incorporating historical and science fiction elements.	His versatility in writing across different genres while maintaining a strong readership and high output of quality work.
Evolved his style dramatically, continuously experimenting and leading major art movements	His ability to continually reinvent his artistic style, influencing multiple art movements and maintaining relevance throughout his career.
Evolved from mathematics and finance to a career focused on invention and innovation, building Amazon and Blue Origin in the process.	His unique path is a combination of long-term vision and patience with extreme focus on experimentation for the benefit of the customer's experience.

As a founder, you get the opportunity to begin again with each new day. Every day brings a point of iteration to rethink and reinvent how you approach one thing, a chance to learn something useful, a chance to become wiser. In fact, the best path for you to choose may not be the most obvious or promising one at any point in time. In my view, the best path is the one that assumes you will keep changing and growing along the way; it's the path that lets you freely evolve, reinvent, learn, and unlearn endlessly.

THE TALE OF THE CUP OF TEA

Nan-in, a Japanese Zen master, received a university professor who came to discuss the principles of Zen. The professor was a reputable expert in his own field, having spent a lifetime picking up opinions and knowledge. Eager to show off his wisdom, he interrupted Nan-in to explain his own views on Zen.

Nan-in served tea. He filled his visitor's cup and then kept pouring. The professor watched the cup overflow until he could no longer restrain himself. "It is overfull. No more will go in," he blurted out.

"Like this cup," Nan-in said, "you are full of your own opinions and speculations. How can I show you Zen unless you first empty your cup?"

On the rugged terrain of entrepreneurship, "being water" isn't just about adapting to circumstances, or even taking advantage of circumstances. Fundamentally, entrepreneurship is about reshaping your circumstances, just like water smooths the hardest of stones.

> *In the pursuit of learning, every day something is acquired. In the pursuit of Tao, every day something is dropped. Less and less is done until non-action is achieved. When nothing is done, nothing is left undone.* —TAO TE CHING

Intentions Define Your Experience

If you want to build a ship, don't drum up people together to collect wood and don't assign them tasks and work, but rather teach them to long for the endless immensity of the sea. —PARAPHRASING ANTOINE DE SAINT-EXUPÉRY

The Buddha taught that all life, including our thoughts, feelings, and actions, arises from our intentions. Right Intention is a core tenet of traditional Buddhist teaching. Right Intention refers to cultivating the correct motivations or mental attitudes that lead to ethical behavior and spiritual growth.

Intentions play such a central role in the perspective from which we experience reality. Sometimes intentions are formed clearly; sometimes they remain unspecified. By being actively mindful of their intentions, founders set up the proper frame of mind for a fulfilling journey. Be intentional about your intentions. As we explored in the section on cultivating agency, framing a challenge as your own deliberate choice can make all the difference.

Being intentional about embracing discomfort, lack of control, and reversals will help you suffer less and grow more. Great founders are willing and able to take on the hardest challenges because they understand how to harness their own intentions to realize their potential.

Filmmaker James Cameron exemplifies this principle through his intentional focus on tackling only the most difficult challenges that no one else dares to take on. Doing the hard things has enabled him to achieve what has never been done before, securing his status as the most commercially successful filmmaker ever.

I believe Cameron understands a powerful truth of the human mind: With time, your ability rises to the level of your intentions. If you focus only on what you perceive as feasible today, you end up selling yourself short in the future. In fact, your intentions can be harnessed for growth. As an example, Cameron worked on *Avatar* for 15 years and *Avatar: The Way of Water* for 12 years. (Most movies take two to three years.) It took him that long because he chose to do things only his future self and future team could accomplish, working persistently over the years to close the gap between present inability and future ability. By deliberately choosing projects that push the boundaries of technology and storytelling, Cameron has continuously set new standards, each movie made possible with technical invention. Thanks to being highly intentional, Cameron is more than willing to embrace the discomfort of the monumental tasks that scare other movie directors away, resulting in unmatched achievements, both artistic and commercial. Cameron has made three of the four biggest box-office successes ever, each bringing in over $2 billion in sales.

Cameron has inspired countless others he has worked with to approach challenges with a similar mindset. With a reputation as someone who takes on big things, he's been able to attract other like-minded people to contribute to making near-impossible movies. He harnessed intentionality for himself, but also for the pursuit of a group endeavor. And that's where most of his leverage comes from—channeling the intentions of a small army of talented, bold, and determined people to make impossible movies together. Cameron taught them to long for the endless immensity of the sea.

Mindful intentions insert meaning into your actions. Meaning is what keeps you going when reason tells you to quit. Meaning keeps you going when others give up. Mindful intention sharpens the blade of your mind, cutting through each challenging moment with finesse and precision. Intentionality lets you assert what you want to experience and position yourself for it.

Harnessing intentions is a skill in itself. Like Cameron, founders can help others define their intentions too by encouraging the team to take on the harder, most meaningful challenges. Your role as a founder and leader is to help others identify and express their purest intentions.

Simple acts done with deep intention

Japanese tea masters set a good example of intentionality in the smallest of actions. As part of the ritual, the tea master selects each utensil with care. Each movement is deliberate, calm, and steady. Through the ritual, the tea master creates an environment of calm and clarity, allowing his guests to fully appreciate the moment's purity and tranquility. This ritual, steeped in centuries of tradition, serves as a daily reminder that intentionality can transform even the simplest of acts into a profound and meaningful experience.

Lastly, cultivate good intentions toward others. Buddhists call this act metta, loosely translated as *loving-kindness.** The simple act of wishing good to others can have a surprisingly positive and powerful effect on the person having the thought, even when

---

* Metta has equivalent concepts in Hinduism, Jainism, and early Vedic texts. For more about the benefits of a metta meditation practice and simple instructions, see this article at Lion's Roar: www.lionsroar.com/metta-meditation-guide.

no words are exchanged. Make kind action a part of your intention.

> *Dark intentions lead to dark results...bright intentions lead to bright results.* —THE BUDDHA

Forging Your Authentic Path: Purpose, People, and Play

The purpose of life is to discover your gift. The meaning of life is to give your gift away.
—DAVID VISCOTT

Living with purpose is one of the finest aspects of entrepreneurship. I personally get a deep sense of harmony and joy when I feel I am contributing what I am meant to be contributing, helping others in my own ways. Great founders are generally able to define their individual purpose with immense clarity. That internal clarity is what enables them to deliver high-quality, impactful work over a long time span.

For most of us, a sense of purpose doesn't just appear one day. Our meaning in the world is discovered gradually and crafted intentionally, with plenty of trials and errors. Clarity that comes with expressing your purpose also brings confidence about what to focus on, and what to let go of. Acting as your inner compass, purpose pushes you to work on yourself as needed, one challenge at a time. That's why some of the very best entrepreneurs seem to be simply unstoppable. And they are unstoppable because there is nothing else they would prefer to be doing than living their authentic purpose.

Polaroid's Edwin Land, who we met in a previous section, is a prime example of a founder nurturing clarity of purpose. As a young boy, he was greatly influenced by Robert Williams Wood's book *Physical Optics*, originally published in 1914, which sparked Land's lifelong interest in optics and photography. Pursuing this natural interest led him to a long career of world-changing inventions, including the instant camera, first produced in 1937. Land kept going back to *Physical Optics* throughout his career. That book, more than anything else, helped him shape his purpose, his own path, by following his childlike curiosity wherever it led him.

Purpose is the ingredient that lets founders tune out the outside noise and expectations in order to gain the mental freedom to do what's right—to express their authentic purpose. As Steve Jobs said, "Don't be trapped by dogma—which is living with the results of other people's thinking." This line is especially important for founders, since entrepreneurs often rely on being contrarian (and right) to win. Having an occupation that requires you to go against convention demands that you think for yourself.

> *The hardest thing is not doing what you want—it's knowing what you want.* —NAVAL RAVIKANT, ANGELLIST CO-FOUNDER

Purpose also has a multiplayer mode

Internal clarity around your individual purpose can also be applied to helping your team find and express a collective purpose—your company's raison d'être, or mission. Companies with a strong sense of purpose tend to have the most success, because it's so much easier for customers, employees, investors, and the general public to understand the mission—and rally behind it.

With a clear purpose, your team will coordinate to create the most authentic version of the work. The reason for your company to exist is so clear and so compelling that customers, employees, and investors know precisely what they're getting into. Because of your reliability, they will feel more trust, which will reinforce their feeling of caring deeply about your mission.

Patagonia's customers understand that the company's mission is to address climate and other environmental issues. What the brand sells is durable, technical outdoor clothing and equipment, but arguably that's not really why people buy the products. Patagonia won their hearts. When people spend money on Patagonia products, they buy the story, the mission. This sense of shared purpose resonates stronger than any ad campaign could.

Founders need to avoid groupthink and peer pressure to follow their authentic purpose. But here's another paradox: We all depend on support and help from others to make our most authentic work happen. If you are going to progress on your purpose and bring it into the real world, someone has to give you money, endorse you, or do you a favor. For example, what's the point of being a painter or a musician if you're not going to share the work? It's the same for founders and for anyone who creates something. While a painter paints and a poet writes for themselves, they also ultimately want to communicate with others, to share a message that resonates. It is a fine balance: Create something for yourself, while making that thing relevant and accessible for others too. Creation is made more meaningful when there is both an object (the work) and a subject to interact with that work. You need other people to progress on your purpose.

The purpose conundrum

Companies always begin as a dream. The founder imagines a future, a vivid and compelling vision that shakes them into chasing their destiny. With time and toil, founders turn their impossible dreams into a lived reality. Caterpillar today, butterfly tomorrow. What begins as a single-minded vision turns into a shared collective dream. Employees, investors, customers—they all start believing in the dream. Each person on the team now contributes small pieces of the collective dream, like ants building a colony. The dream might be born out of the founder(s), but it is raised and nurtured by the company.

At this point of your founder journey, you must let your dream go in order to let it grow. Others will appropriate, redefine, and riff on your version of the dream. As you become one of many contributors to that dream, it can be very hard to let go.

What happens when purpose at the collective level evolves in a way that does not match the founder's individual purpose? Founders sometimes let their individual purpose take a back seat for a while because they want to ensure their company does everything to make the collective dream a reality. Your company comes before you, and you make personal sacrifices because of your commitment. All founders experience this at some point. The separation of your own sense of purpose and your company's purpose may have happened slowly and gradually, but you didn't notice until that separation became evident. Maybe you feel like you lost sight of yourself for a while.

Steve Jobs was famously fired from Apple in 1985 as a result of his differing views on what the company needed. His calling, his purpose and meaning, was to design "insanely great products," which he believed was also Apple's purpose. But at that point in time, the board and the new CEO had other views. Excellent products and technical prowess were not their dream, and they found Jobs brash and difficult. His style, in addition to his different vision of the future for Apple, led to his firing.

Today it is obvious that Jobs's dream was the most authentic contribution he could make to Apple. When he returned to the company in 1997, he was humbled and a more effective leader, with an improved ability to motivate people. The second time around, Jobs was more self-aware—he had learned the lessons he needed to learn. He was able to keep his individual and Apple's purposes in harmony. He had solved his purpose conundrum. His vision of building insanely great products resumed, and soon magic returned to Apple.

Founders are expected to place the company first. To be the last person to leave the ship. Selfless sacrifice is what we think leadership is made of, that a leader's duty is to be totally committed to doing what is best for the group, no matter the personal cost. But this is not entirely a black-and-white thing. Chronic tension between your personal sense of purpose and the company's needs can impair your leadership. When you're no longer free to be authentic, your spirit starts to decay.

Founders end up leaving or being fired from the company they created because of the purpose conundrum, because they are unable to reconcile individual and collective dreams. Yet without prioritizing their individual purpose, founders struggle to contribute and be happy in their demanding role. They lose their meaning. They lose their way.

So how can you keep your individual and collective purpose in harmony? Through play.

Find authenticity through play

> *You want to find something that looks like work to others, but feels like play to you.* —NAVAL RAVIKANT

One of the main reasons founders struggle with purpose is that they forget to play. Edwin Land remained that curious child as he created instant photography. Same with Jobs crafting the next Apple products. Play solves the purpose conundrum: Find ways to play at work, even if they don't seem like the best use of your time. Take a small amount of time and make a ritual of following your curiosity for curiosity's sake. It's hard to worry about purpose when you are playing—just look at children immersed in play to see how present and authentic they are.

I hope I'm not the first one to tell you that you're much more likely to stick with something you genuinely enjoy. Although work certainly won't always be fun, approaching it with a spirit of playfulness and curiosity will fuel creativity and innovation. It will keep you interested and engaged. Competition will have a hard time keeping up: They are working while you're playing.

> *Don't aim to be the best, be the only.* —KEVIN KELLY, FOUNDER OF *WIRED* MAGAZINE

Pain Is Inevitable, Suffering Is Optional

Excellence is the capacity to endure pain. —ISADORE SHARP, FOUNDER OF FOUR SEASONS HOTELS AND RESORTS

For most humans, emotions and behaviors are ruled by the dual perspective of pain vs. pleasure. There's an obvious reason why living creatures are wired to avoid pain, discomfort, and inconvenience: Difficult emotions play a role in natural evolution. But in modern life, moving toward a degree of pain can be a very good thing.

Of course pain, and how you approach pain, is a crucial aspect of the work of a founder—and anyone attempting to do difficult, meaningful, and creative work. Noticing and responding to pain is a skill in itself. How do you relate to your own discomfort? Do you stay with it, or do you try to make it go away? Being in an emotional position to move toward the pain when everyone else is running for the exits makes you the best kind of contrarian there is—a resilient one.

An essential aspect of being a successful founder comes down to your ability to endure emotional hardships. Leaning into adversity today better equips you to handle more adversity tomorrow; the habit of overriding your inner demons and leaning into mental discomfort becomes progressively easier with time. The wisest among us understand that they can harness their pain and pleasure instead of being gripped by them.

James Dyson spent close to 20 years going from failure to failure as an inventor. Much of that time he was in heavy personal debt, with a family to support, a mortgage to pay, and no money. He made over 5,000 failed prototypes of what would become the Dyson Dual Cyclone, a bagless vacuum cleaner, during which time he fought a stream of lawsuits for patent infringement.

At last, when the Dual Cyclone launched, its phenomenal success redeemed him and made all of the pain and failures worth it. I doubt I would have had the mental strength to continue trying as long as Dyson did. What made this man so willing and able to handle such adversity, and for that long? Dyson dealt with the pain that comes from trying to do something new, as well as the internal struggles—the doubts, the sacrifices, the regrets, and missed opportunities. How did Dyson do it?

The answer is a challenge-centric mindset. Dyson grew up as a competitive runner, which taught him invaluable lessons when it comes to training, as shared in his autobiography *Against the Odds*:

> There was no one to teach me how to run. There was no dad to tell me how great I was, and it became a very introverted kind of obsession with me. Herb Elliot was a big name at the time, so I read a few books about him and discovered that his coach had told him that the way to develop

stamina and strengthen the leg muscles was to run up and down sand dunes.

The act of running itself was not something I enjoyed. The best you could say for it was that it was lonely and painful. But as I started to win by greater and greater margins I did it more and more, because I knew the reason for my success was that out on the sand dunes I was doing something that no one else was doing. Apart from me and Herb, no one knew. They were all running round and round the track like a herd of sheep and not getting any quicker. Difference itself was making me come first.[*]

He later explained in an interview in *Runner's World*:

What I've learned from running is that the time to push hard is when you're hurting like crazy and you want to give up. The moment you should accelerate is the moment you're the most tired. The beginning of the final lap is the testing point, and so I found that to be in life. Success is often just

---

[*] Dyson *Against the Odds*, 89.

around the corner. You might make a discovery. You might call it obstinacy or determination. It almost made me sort of relish that moment. I see it as an opportunity, that point where if you know you can get through that bit, you're going to make an important discovery that someone else might have made except they gave up, because they couldn't get through the difficulties. I got that from running.[*]

Dyson relished challenge and hardship as a way to stand apart from the rest. He embraced the pain because he knew what lay on the other side of it. That said, leaning into pain doesn't mean you need to suffer endlessly.

THE TALE OF THE SECOND ARROW

The Buddha asked his student, "If I strike you with an arrow, will it be painful?" The student replied, "Yes." The Buddha then asked, "If I strike you with a second arrow, in the same spot, is it

---

[*] Averett, "I'm a Runner"

even more painful?" The student again replied, "Yes, of course, it would be incredibly more painful than the first arrow."

The Buddha then explained that in life, the first arrow represents the initial pain that we experience from external events, which is inevitable. The second arrow represents the additional suffering we inflict upon ourselves through our reactions to these events, such as anger, worry, resentment, or self-pity. This second arrow is more subjective—it is experienced from within, through our thoughts and emotions. In other words, suffering comes from your mind, not the outside world. Therefore, your suffering is more optional than you think.

Speaking for myself, I've noticed that suffering usually tags along with anticipation. I anticipate something bad will happen in the future, and I suffer right now as a result of a hypothetical, sometimes unlikely problem that only exists in my mind. In the meantime, nothing about my present reality has changed.

There are more things likely to frighten us than to crush us....We suffer more often in imagination than reality. —SENECA

Researchers at Penn State University asked a cohort of people with generalized anxiety disorder to write down everything they worried about for a period of a month. The participants also recorded how things played out against the worries they had. The researchers found that 91 percent of the participants' worries didn't come true. For several study participants, exactly zero of the things that they worried about actually happened. Of the few who saw their worries materialize, 79 percent discovered they could handle the difficulty better than expected, or that the event taught them a lesson worth learning. In other words, the worst case wasn't nearly as bad as they had expected.[*] Worry is a contagious emotion. And so is calmness. As a founder, which emotions do you want your team to pick up on?

---

[*] LaFreniere and Newman, "Exposing Worry's Deceit."

Discomfort helps your future self

Leaning into pain means getting comfortable with being uncomfortable. What thoughts and emotions are you avoiding because they seem unbearable? Opening up to the feelings you don't want to feel is a first courageous step. Acknowledging the discomfort that comes from looking in the dark corners of your mind, where you don't want to ever visit, helps make those demons much less powerful. By being emotionally truthful about your repressed emotions, you'll be positioned to face your demons head-on, and free yourself, emotionally speaking.

Leaning into discomfort can often be framed as an *investment*. The discomfort may lead to greatness and meaning. Even if it doesn't, you still come out stronger and learn something along the way. Proactive pain management is at the core of a growth mindset. Consider that you're doing your future self a favor by choosing the harder way today. "All self-help boils down to 'choose long-term over short-term,'" said Naval Ravikant. That's why grit and determination are key aspects of founder psychology—they are the investments you make into your future self.

I've learned that what makes a successful entrepreneur is the same thing that makes a good skateboarder or good surfer: You need grit and determination to get back up every time you're knocked off the board. —PAUL VAN DOREN, FOUNDER OF VANS

Paradoxically, the more difficult something is to attain, the more it is worth pursuing. I enjoy surfing because it is hard, and I fail at riding the wave most of the time. It's good mental conditioning to push myself to deal with repeated failure on a small scale. It makes the occasional waves I catch so rewarding, not unlike entrepreneurship. I know I wouldn't enjoy surfing nearly as much if it was easier. If you do only one thing as a founder, learn to handle more discomfort—this will propel you immensely on your founder journey.

It's not the load that breaks you down; it's the way you carry it.
—LOU HOLTZ, FOOTBALL COACH

Your Beliefs Are Assumptions to Be Tested

It ain't what you don't know that gets you into trouble. It's what you know for sure that just ain't so.

—MARK TWAIN

Your most dangerous beliefs are the ones you are completely confident of. Certainty makes you unaware of what you do not know. It keeps you from seeking the newer and better information that would contradict your beliefs. This high sense of certainty is overconfidence bias; it makes you mentally rigid, unable to see the big picture or think the unthinkable. Complete certainty leaves you completely exposed when your beliefs turn out to be false.

For example, in the late 2000s, Research in Motion (RIM), the creator of BlackBerry phones, was the undisputed leader in the smartphone market. RIM didn't consider Apple's new iPhone a serious threat to their enterprise customer base. RIM executives believed that the iPhone's virtual keyboard would be less efficient than BlackBerry's physical one, which was then a core feature for BlackBerry users. They also viewed the iPhone's power and data usage as just too large to be practical. They did not believe Apple could offer reliable and efficient email service, another RIM asset. RIM prided itself on the security of its devices and believed Apple could not match them.

Overconfidence led RIM's leadership to under-react to an existential threat. They became so sure of themselves that they forgot to ask "What if we're wrong?" They responded to the tectonic shift in the smartphone market by focusing on small, incremental improvements to their existing products. RIM believed that maintaining its strengths, such as battery life and the physical keyboard, was enough to fend off Apple. But this was not a feature-by-feature battle for who had the best phone—Apple's design led to a profound cultural shift in consumers, and RIM completely missed it. Apple changed consumers' ideas about what represents a seamless experience by integrating the hardware and software with Apple's operating system—something no other phone makers had done. By controlling the entire user experience, Apple was able to draw people to form completely new phone habits and expectations.

With time, the features RIM offered became progressively less attractive to consumers, and the company faded away. The hubris was obvious: In 2007, the year the first Apple smartphone launched, RIM's co-CEO Jim Basillie appeared in the news not to talk about Blackberry, but to talk about the hockey teams he was trying to buy with his fortune. In hindsight, he should have been fighting for the survival of the company. We know how the story ends: It was certainty, not curiosity, that killed the cat.

Throughout history, the patterns are clear and consistent: Certainty and complacency make a bad strategy in a dynamic world ruled by constant change. RIM is one small example of endless mistakes caused by overconfidence. Kodak missed the boat on digital photography. Blockbuster overlooked Netflix. RadioShack and Toys R Us didn't see Amazon coming until it was too late. A fatal sin founders commit is to remain in denial of existential threats. As Andy Grove, co-founder of Intel famously said, "Only the paranoid survive."

Overconfidence is a timeless human theme. Ancient civilizations have collapsed under the weight of their own entitlement. An abundance of resources breeds inertia, giving people a sense of comfort and invincibility. But having more land, more people, and more money requires more coordination across the empire. Endless expansion inevitably reaches a point where it becomes harder to maintain those ever-rising living standards. That's why winning can be risky: You lower your guard and get fat and comfortable. When you haven't lost lately, you start to assume you can't lose. This is hubris. Your size and reputation that once served you eventually hold you back. Soon enough, hungry, determined competitors will catch up to you, then topple you. They have little to lose while you have everything to lose.

Many founders embrace the ethos of "thinking big"—a good intention that can also become a trap: You become overconfident, thinking so big that you overreach. Thinking big shouldn't lead to delusion. Let the lessons of history be your guide. A more appropriate mantra for founders: "Think big, with just the right amount of confidence." Less catchy, more helpful for survival. The difference between confidence and overconfidence is the hubris that comes from a sense of superiority and entitlement. The line between the two can be thin, but it is a critical one for founders to keep in mind.

Don't confuse what you want to be true with what truly is

Overconfidence bias is one form of faulty belief. Another common way we deceive ourselves is to believe *what we want to be true*, as opposed to *what is actually true*. We tend to do this because of confirmation bias—we overvalue evidence that confirms our existing views, and overlook facts that threaten our position. Instead of embracing all facts and shaping our beliefs based on reality, our confirmation bias makes us try to shape reality to fit our beliefs. Being wrong shakes our ego, our core identity. That's why seeking the truth can be so uncomfortable, even unbearable for some.

A tragic example of confirmation bias is the story of Dr. Ignaz Semmelweis's theory that handwashing could save lives by preventing germs from spreading. Semmelweis observed that the death rate from childbed fever was much higher in the maternity ward staffed by doctors and medical students than in the ward staffed by midwives. Semmelweis hypothesized that the doctors and students, who often came directly from autopsies, were transmitting some kind of contamination to the mothers. In 1847, Semmelweis implemented a policy requiring doctors and students to wash their hands with a solution of chlorinated lime for before examining pregnant women. This practice led to a significant reduction in the incidence of childbed fever in his ward.

Yet Semmelweis's findings were largely ignored, ridiculed, or rejected by the medical establishment. The lack of a theoretical explanation for his observations—the germ theory of disease was not yet widely accepted—hindered his efforts to convince his peers. It wasn't until years after his death, when germ theory was proven by the work of scientists like Louis Pasteur and Joseph Lister, that Semmelweis's recommendations for hand hygiene became a standard—and critically important—practice in medicine.

Doctors had a clear incentive to adopt handwashing, given that it worked and cost almost nothing. Yet they stubbornly refused to change their ways, costing countless lives in the process. Why did Semmelweis's recommendation, backed with evidence, take 40 years to become widely accepted? Because humans struggle to accept as true the things they don't understand, even when the data is clear. Again, seeking the truth is just too uncomfortable, and it sometimes seems easier to just avoid it.

Don't assume that things can't be true just because you don't understand the logic behind them, or because you're deeply invested in your own view. The truth is still the truth whether you think it is or not, and whether it suits you or not. Making the best decisions and getting the best outcomes requires the courage to actively scrutinize and replace your faulty beliefs—especially the ones that seem most solid.

Beliefs are hypotheses to be tested, not treasures to be guarded. —PHILIP TETLOCK

Great founders are usually able to counterargue their own positions. Doing so requires that you don't trust too much in your own beliefs, so that you can reconcile opposing perspectives. Great founders don't let their original beliefs get in the way of finding better ones. Scrutinizing your beliefs takes humility and honesty.

In fact, you can intentionally harness opposing perspectives with your team. The healthy tension that comes from differing beliefs can lead to better decisions. You gain a shared clarity around the issue at hand by hearing how different people see it and would tackle it. The very act of discussing where perspectives differ often leads to a new and better solution, essentially a third option that combines the best of the original arguments. Research shows that healthy tension tends to lead to better decisions than polite agreement.

Jeff Bezos took this approach of welcoming competing perspectives in 2005 when deciding whether to launch Amazon Prime. Today Prime has over 200 million members and is credited for pioneering the "next day, free shipping" customer promise. In 2005, free and fast shipping were not yet common e-commerce practices, and many Amazon finance executives did not see how the company could afford such a wild promise. Some found it absurd that users would pay for a premium delivery experience. As obvious as the decision looks today, Prime was highly debated among Amazon teams. Bezos encouraged all the opposing perspectives he could from his team, and he listened carefully. Eventually he came to believe that higher customer satisfaction and long-term loyalty would justify the investment in Prime's free next-day shipping offer.

As a way to make the Prime membership profitable rapidly and to reduce risk, Amazon bundled Prime with additional free services at zero marginal cost, including music and video. By doing this, Bezos justified the enormous capital investment needed to promise fast and free delivery by creating the right conditions for frequent customer touchpoints, increasing the share of attention Amazon gets from its customers. As a result, these customers were trained to use Amazon products more often, spending much more money as a result. The average Amazon customer more than doubled their total Amazon spending after signing up for Prime, and the product has an annual renewal rate of over 90 percent.

Initially, the Amazon teams had not considered the third option for Prime, which was to bundle the delivery promise with so much value already available within Amazon. They could not see how customer spending behavior would change as a result of capturing more of their attention. Today most Prime members would tell you that the membership pays for itself, making it a no-brainer. Bezos was right in harnessing conflicting views at the beginning. Sitting with the apparent contradictions for a while helped him find a fresh, optimal solution that gave Amazon a deep strategic advantage.

A changing world is no place for rigid beliefs

Holding onto your solid beliefs in a fast-changing world is absurd. Yet, we all tend to do this as we try to protect our ego. I've noticed my ego comes out whenever someone challenges a belief I value. I can get too invested in being right, leading to me feeling offended. I become rigid when I identify with my beliefs, and I get caught up in strong emotions because of my strong opinions. For me, feeling offended has become a signal to curb my ego. Only by taming my ego can I let go of my problematic beliefs.

Buddhists teach that the path to inner peace is to not identify too strongly with your thoughts and emotions. The same goes for your beliefs: They are just thoughts. It is up to you whether these thoughts become your identity. You are not your beliefs and opinions, and identifying with them will cause you to suffer. It is better hold them loosely.

Consider what happens when, inevitably, you are wrong. Can you survive being wrong, no matter how confident you are right now? Being wrong will only ruin you if you go emotionally all in. Moderating your beliefs by keeping a healthy mental distance and readily discarding them when it's appropriate makes it easier to shed the false beliefs holding you back and replace them with better ones. As a founder, you will be more effective by preemptively acknowledging the downsides of your beliefs, no matter how certain you are, than by digging your heels in and trying to prove the validity of your beliefs. Treat your beliefs as assumptions to be tested. When handled well, being wrong will let you grow tremendously.

How you think matters more than what you think. —PHILIP TETLOCK

10,000 Iterations

I have not failed. I've just found
10,000 ways that won't work.
—THOMAS EDISON

You've likely heard that it takes 10,000 hours of practice to become a world-class expert in your field of choice. This idea was originally shared by Malcolm Gladwell in his book *Outliers: The Story of Success*. Although the 10,000 hours theory makes sense, people tend to miss the real point of it. The *amount* of time you put in counts less than the *quality* of each hour of work you put in. What you do during those hours is what truly matters.

For that reason, when it comes to mastering the craft of entrepreneurship, I've found that 10,000 *iterations* is a better measure of progress than 10,000 hours. Thomas Edison iterated over 10,000 prototypes of various inventions—and holds a record 1,093 patents under his name. Those patents include the phonograph, the electric lightbulb, and the storage battery. James Dyson, as we saw earlier, iterated over 5,000 prototypes before launching his first bagless vacuum cleaner. The Wright brothers' first airplane, James Dewar's Thermos flask, Graham Bell's telephone, and Edwin Land's instant camera each required over 1,000 iterations before gaining mass appeal.

Most iterations do not produce genuine breakthroughs. They provide subtle and marginal improvements. Still, those small changes compound as you spend time learning your field of choice, guided by a trial-and-error process, pushing the boundary of your expertise, year after year.

Some aspects of your life can and should be approached with maximal efficiency, like managing email for example. But when it comes to developing your craft, efficiency is *not* the way to go. There are no shortcuts. Real craftsmanship requires the inefficiency of iterations. Craftsmanship is inefficient because there are no paved routes to get to the very top in terms of quality and excellence—just like you can't just drive your car up Mount Everest. Craftsmanship, by definition, cannot be mass-produced. You have to earn your craft. This is the case for mastering any field, whether you are a Swiss watchmaker, an Olympic athlete, or an entrepreneur. You have to spend the years forging your route to greatness. You will have some help, but it is up to you to figure out your blueprint to mastery. There are no shortcuts.

In order words, you can't just clock in your 10,000 hours as efficiently as possible and passively expect greatness. This is not math. You can't compensate for sloppy work by doing more of it. Deliberate and tedious practice is what actually helps you improve. Paradoxically, you get better faster by relishing the hard and boring work while others are looking for shortcuts. Very few people have the mindset to keep doing *just one thing*, fully dedicated to their craft, for 10 years or more. Patience will always be in short supply. But with enough time, even the smallest of improvements stack up to tangible breakthroughs. As a craftsman, as a maker, doing the inefficient work is what sets you up for what isn't attainable today.

What you choose to work on, and who you choose to work with, are far more important than how hard you work. —NAVAL RAVIKANT

To me, having the chance to work on meaningful and creative challenges, with friends inspiring each other, is entrepreneurship's greatest privilege. Once you know your direction, and who to go with, then it all comes down to focus—applying time, effort, and deep care toward reaching your dream. People are much better at thinking linearly than thinking exponentially (calculus, a branch of mathematics covering exponentials, happens to be the high school subject with the highest failure rate). Consistent focus is an advantage hidden in plain sight. It is immensely challenging to focus on just one thing and stick to it for years while the world around you is screaming for your attention. Most people quit too soon because they get discouraged or bored; they change their priorities midcourse, mistakenly thinking their approach is not working. But all they had to do was keep focused long enough to let the compounding work. Getting results always seems to take longer than imagined. But that's not a reason to stop.

> *The first rule of compounding:*
> *Never interrupt it unnecessarily.*
> — CHARLIE MUNGER

THE TALE OF THE CLEVER
GIRL AND THE GREEDY RAJA

In a small Indian village, a clever young girl found herself facing a greedy raja during a time of famine. The raja was hoarding all the city's rice reserves, unwilling to help his people. As a way to save the people around her, the young girl asked the raja for just one grain of rice, doubled each day, for 30 days. The raja agreed without hesitation.

As the days passed, the raja began to realize what he'd gotten into. By the end of the month, the exponential growth of the rice amounted to 77 tons, emptying his reserves. The wise girl understood the power of compounding and ensured that the people received the food they needed.

This tale shows how difficult it is for the human mind to grasp the sheer power of exponential growth, and just how powerful a daily streak can become. Consistent focus is the magic ingredient of compounding.

The five-hour rule

An uninterrupted daily streak is all it takes for compounding to take off, assuming you persist long enough to get results. Getting the benefits of consistency is about making the time, usually three to five hours, to focus on the hardest and most creative part of your job—and to prioritize it every day. Productivity researcher Anders Ericsson found that the top performers in various fields seem to max out at three to five hours of creative work daily. For example, he notes that many established authors "tend to write only 4 hours per day, leaving the rest of the day for rest and recuperation." He also found that the top violinists at a prestigious music college practiced, on average, 3.5 hours per day.[*]

Meaningful creative work is tiring. Because of the intense concentration needed for creative work, I usually run out of mental fuel before I run out of time. When you're doing something challenging, it is better to manage your energy than your time.

Feeling tired, unmotivated, or distracted is also part of the course. Expect it. Plan for it. Five hours leaves room for distractions to come up during the rest of your day, because whether important or trivial, some random things will undoubtedly demand your attention. Give yourself a buffer, a dedicated time to be less effective. Block out those five hours, then leave the remainder of your day open for anything else that

---

[*] Ericsson, Krampe, and Tesch-Romer, "Acquisition of Expert Performance."

comes up, which is time that can be adapted based on your mood, energy, or interests of the day.

You can't do five hours? No problem—start small and work your way up. As Greg McKeown, author of *Essentialism: The Disciplined Pursuit of Less* suggests, block out two hours to work on a single goal. Use this time to work on your most important priority for the day, the month, the year. If needed, start with as little as 15 minutes. Just start blocking time and aim to expand.

In the context of entrepreneurship, five hours of creative work can look like coding, designing a new product, talking to customers, or researching your market for insights. Internal meetings are generally useless for creative work, but they can help organize teams to work better. In general, I find that meetings do not have the same creative output as asynchronous, hands-on tasks. There are always exceptions of course, but usually deep creativity aligns with solitude.

Many creative masters have embraced their own version of the five-hour rule. Stephen King writes around five hours per day, as does J. K. Rowling. Jerry Seinfeld too. Arnold Schwarzenegger trained as a bodybuilder for five hours per day, and later trained to become an actor for five hours per day. Leonardo da Vinci, Paul Graham, Winston Churchill—the list of people who claim to be a part of the five-hour club goes on.

> *Intense concentration...can bring out resources in people that they didn't know they had.* —EDWIN LAND

Believing in your creative process is a key ingredient for consistency and focus. The initial period, when you start putting in effort but have yet to see any results, is going to test your resolve. That is true especially when you're creating something never done before. Although you never know how new things will turn out, consistency inevitably speaks for itself. Sticking with the process is what makes you creative. The more you believe this statement is true, that your success is unavoidable and solely a matter of time provided you focus consistently, the more likely you are to stick to your goals. Trust the creative process and it will guide you.

Also, choosing consistent focus over hard grind also means you can relax for the same result.[*] You're going to do and feel a lot better when you enjoy the journey instead of straining so much.

> *I fear not the man who has practiced 10,000 kicks once, but I fear the man who has practiced one kick 10,000 times.* —BRUCE LEE

---

[*] Derek Sivers has a great passage about this in his book *Hell Yeah or No*, and you can read the excerpt on his website: https://sive.rs/relax.

Your Goals Define Who You Become

No dream is as great as the person you might become by remaining true to it. —DEE HOCK, FOUNDER OF VISA

As we touched on earlier, knowing what to focus on is a hard question all founders grapple with. After all, entrepreneurship is an open-ended adventure with no fixed rules. The only rules that apply to you are the ones you decide work for you.

With no explicit rules, and with the definition of success being entirely subjective, the role of the founder is, by definition, ambiguous, complex, and demanding. It's hard to decide what to prioritize when there seems to be so many important ways to use your time. As we've seen in the last section, focus, especially intense focus, is such a critical skill for founders to reach full potential.

Founders who hold extreme focus by doing just one main thing tend to have the most impact. This is a trait I've noticed among the best founders in history.* They are able to remove all distractions. But perhaps even more powerful, this level of focus and clarity becomes a cultural norm within the company. Founders with mixed priorities end up leading a confused team building the wrong things. As HP co-founder David Packard elegantly put it, "More businesses die from indigestion than starvation."†

Steve Jobs was focused on one thing: great design. Unsurprisingly, Apple has a streamlined and integrated product suite. Jeff Bezos focused on customer

---

* Sadly, extreme focus can become neglect when taken to an extreme; unsurprisingly, many celebrity founders have dysfunctional personal lives. The real heroes are the ones who manage to build a great business AND a house full of love.

† Packard, *The HP Way*.

obsession; Amazon became known for innovating on behalf of customers, steadily improving the experience throughout the years. Google creators Larry Page and Sergey Brin had an extreme focus on organizing the internet and making it accessible. Beyond its search engine, Google has pioneered seemingly disjointed products, but they all have the same focus: Maps, Books, Analytics, and Translate all help organize online data and make it usable.

> *An organization's focus rests on its leader's ability to focus.* —PAUL VAN DOREN

Vans founder Paul Van Doren exemplifies this kind of focused leadership. "What I do better than anything else is cut out distractions," he wrote in his memoir, *Authentic.* "If a system isn't working efficiently, I can see where it's jammed, eliminate the problem, and find a way to keep everything moving forward. Everyone has something they naturally do better than anyone else—this happens to be mine, and I was lucky enough to have the opportunity to leverage it for myself and others."[*]

Goals are about more than making your focus explicit. To me, the higher reason for having goals is not to be productive or successful, but to decide who you want to be, and what you really value. What you focus on consistently through the years will define your impact, your character, and ultimately your legacy.

In setting goals, most people think of what to do or what they want to have. Few people consider the person they become in pursuing a goal. Goals are typically focused on changing something; therefore, it seems sensible for you to change along the way. The best goals center on *becoming*, not doing or having. That's because the most rewarding aspects of reaching your goal lie in your chance at improving, each step of the way.

Some goals will bring you permanent value, while others will only bring you ephemeral satisfaction. "Be" goals stay with you, while "do" and "have" goals are temporary. For example, if you want to improve your health, you can choose to become a healthier person (be) or to

---

[*] Van Doren, *Authentic*, xiii.

lose weight (do). Most people focus on losing weight without a change in their identity because it seems the simpler or faster approach; then they end up gaining back the weight they lose. A "be" goal is better because once the weight has been lost, the change in habits and identity that gave you the results remains in place.

"BE" VS. "HAVE" GOALS FOR FOUNDERS

BE GOALS	DO/HAVE GOALS
Embody authenticity in all business endeavors with a message that resonates	Reach 1 million social media followers
Develop more empathy and context from employees and customers	Open 10 new retail locations in the next 2 years
Genuinely engage toward social impact and community betterment	Increase employee retention rate by 10 percent
Be more nimble, able to experiment, and ship small and fast	Launch a new product line by the end of Q3
Be a visionary leader who inspires innovation	Expand the company's market share by 20 percent within a year

THE TALE OF THE MONK AND
THE CRYSTAL MOUNTAIN

A monk heard of a legendary Crystal Mountain at the far end of a vast desert, full of jewels. Believing he could use the wealth to fund monasteries and help the needy, he set off on a long journey. He faced burning sun, freezing nights, and sandstorms, helping other travelers in need along the way.

Eventually, the monk reached Crystal Mountain, its beauty beyond imagination. As he meditated, he realized his true treasure was not the crystals but the inner strength, patience, and compassion he gained on his journey.

Taking a single crystal as a token, the monk returned to teach others about the wealth found in resilience, kindness, compassion, and self-discovery.

This tale shows transformation in the pursuit of goals. Once the monk reached Crystal Mountain, he discovered that the reward was not the wealth he sought, but the inner growth he experienced along the way. He understood that the meaning of the goal lies in the personal transformation that the journey brings.

It's hard to know why you want what you want

Given our mimetic nature, it is essential as a founder to be able to discern whether your goals are coming from within or from outside yourself. Without introspection it is easy to inadvertently adopt others' beliefs or desires. That's why knowing why you want what you want is the best way to remain true to yourself.

How do you know if your goals are truly authentic and intrinsic? For me, looking at them through the lens of time travel greatly helps me focus on becoming who I really want to become, with confidence and clarity, regardless of the noise that is external reality. Following are examples of questions you can ask yourself to frame your goals with a time travel perspective.

- **Will this goal matter in 10 years?** Discard goals without a clear picture of what changes will look like down the line. Most things you are concerned with today won't matter when you look back.

- **What would your 80-year-old self think?** How might you feel looking back? Will you regret more what you did or what you did not do?

- **What would your 15-year-old self think?** Would your young self be happy, disappointed, or surprised with your adult choices?

Being ambitious, many founders try to manifest the most extreme version of their goals. But making a goal bigger isn't necessarily better. Size can distract from what truly matters, like who you are and who you will become by pursuing your goals. If size means you can help more people or make a bigger contribution to your mission, and your mission is authentic and for the greater good, then by all means maximize your goals. But size for its own sake is not a valid goal.

A clear view of who you want to become lets you embrace the "less-is-more" mantra. By doing less, you do what you do, only better. By wanting less, you give life more flavor and more presence for the fewer things you do really want and value. Check your desires. Desiring less and desiring better lead to a peaceful mind—and perhaps clearer goals.

Goals shouldn't feel like an impossible burden that makes your life hard; they should make you feel more alive by giving you focus and energy. All worthy goals take hard work and sacrifice, but being consistently depressed or anxious about reaching your goal is a sign you might be reaching for the wrong things in the wrong way. Feeling burdened by your goals is a nudge to consider other goals that will make you feel more alive and allow you to fully engage in the present as you pursue them.

THE TALE OF THE FISHERMAN AND THE BUSINESSMAN

An executive of a large, public company was on (a rare) vacation in a small coastal village when he saw a fisherman docking his boat. Inside the boat were several large fish. Impressed, the businessman asked the fisherman how long it took to catch them. "Only a little while."

The businessman then asked why he didn't stay out longer to catch more fish. The fisherman explained that he had enough to support his family's immediate needs. The businessman pressed on, asking what the fisherman did with the rest of his time. The fisherman said, "I sleep late, fish a little, play with my children, take siestas with my wife, and stroll into the village each evening where I sip wine and play guitar with my friends. I have a full and busy life."

The executive scoffed and offered a business plan: "I built and sold companies for a lot of money, and I could help you. You should spend more time fishing, and with the proceeds buy a bigger boat. With the proceeds from the bigger boat, you could buy several boats, and eventually you would have a whole fleet of fishing boats. Instead of selling your catch to a middleman, you could sell directly to the processor, eventually opening your own cannery. You would control the product, processing, and distribution. You would need to leave this small coastal fishing village and move to a bigger village, then the next bigger village, and eventually the big city, where you will run your expanding enterprise."

"How long will this all take?" the fisherman asked.

"Fifteen to twenty years. Twenty-five tops."

"And then what?"

The executive laughed and said, "That's the best part. When the time is right, you would announce an IPO and sell your company stock to the public and become very rich. You would make billions."

"Billions? Then what?"

"Then you would retire," the businessman said. "Move to a small coastal fishing village where you would sleep late, fish a little, play with your kids, take siestas with your wife, and stroll to the village in the evenings where you could sip wine and play your guitar with your friends."

Big goals mean little if they aren't aligned with what you value most. The person you become in pursuing your goals is more important than whether you succeed in achieving the goals. Great goals can certainly lead you to become a great person. But although goals exist in the future, they should help you be a more fulfilled and upgraded version of yourself *today* and along the way.

The downside of goals

Beware: While goals can motivate you to push yourself to reach a greater potential, they can also, paradoxically, make you feel inadequate. Embedded in goals is the implicit notion that things can, and should, be improved. Goals expose a gap in your reality; they are inherently a desire to change something that comes from the observation that things are not as good as they could be.

Goals can make you greedy. Perhaps the biggest downside of chasing your goals is how difficult it is to stop the goalpost from moving after you reach the initial target. While humans innately seek to push our limits, a sense of having and being enough is the highest form of wealth one can have. That feeling of contentment can only come from within.

> *The wealthiest person is a pauper at times / compared to the man with a satisfied mind.* —JOHNNY CASH, "SATISFIED MIND"

Lastly, fixating on your goals can become a form of escapism, a way to bypass the present for a brighter (yet still imaginary) future. You are fooling yourself if you think you need to reach your goals to allow yourself to feel good about yourself. Many founders, including me, are naturally future oriented instead of present oriented.* Future orientation is great for planning and achieving, a great mindset for achievement—but not so great for contentment. Don't use goals to escape from a today you wish was entirely

---

* Derek Sivers discusses this idea in his post "Are You Present-Focused or Future-Focused?": https://sive.rs/time.

different. Create goals that start with your current reality, and build with it.

Choose goals that minimize future regrets

Fast-forward to the end of your life. What will you think as you look back on your entire journey? Consider the regrets your future self may face in your final days. In her book *The Top Five Regrets of the Dying: A Life Transformed by the Dearly Departing,* Bronnie Ware writes about the regrets dying patients reported during her time working in palliative care. According to Ware, the top five regrets people had on their deathbeds were:

- I wish I had the courage to live a life that was true to myself, not the life others expected of me.

- I wish I had not worked so hard.

- I wish I had the courage to express my feelings.

- I wish I had stayed in touch with my friends.

- I wish I had let myself be happier.[*]

---

[*] See more on her blog: https://bronnieware.com/blog/regrets -of-the-dying.

This perspective cuts to the core of what life is really about. There is no mention of money, fame, status, or power. None of that matters in the end. No one else can evaluate your goals. Goals are a very personal thing. You don't have to share them with anyone else. In fact, it might be a great idea to not tell anyone. When you hold these truths privately, it is easier to stay true to yourself. It is also easier to change them.

But doesn't discarding goals mean you're a quitter? Shouldn't you tell others your goals so they can keep you accountable? Here lies another conundrum founders encounter: the choice of when to persevere and when to pick another goal. There are valid arguments on either side for making your goals public or private. In any case, the key when changing goals is replacing them with *improved* goals, not abandoning them outright just because they are hard. Change goals only to upgrade them.

Having your own inner scorecard takes courage. It takes courage to trust your inner voice and take unpopular action. What others think of you is not up to you. It is also none of your business. A life well lived includes a healthy distance from what other people think. When it comes to defining your own life, you are the coach, the player, and the referee. You're also the post-game commentator, the season-ticket holder, the cheerleader, and the fluffy mascot. Goals start and end with you.

> *I always wanted to be somebody, but now I realize I should have been more specific.* —LILY TOMLIN

Strength in Systems

The system, to a large extent, causes its own behavior. —DONELLA MEADOWS, AUTHOR OF *THINKING IN SYSTEMS*

The popular notion of productivity has been shifting away from goals and toward systems in recent years. Some productivity experts now declare goals useless. While there is plenty of sense in focusing on systems to get things done, I don't think systems can replace goals. Your systems produce deliberate and consistent action that fuels your progress, but systems don't give you a direction. As we've seen, goals are key to defining who you want to become. Goals and systems serve different purposes, and I believe in combining them for maximum effect. Why take a dual view by choosing one over the other? Embrace both.

Systems are the tools that let you automate, simplify, and keep the cadence on your way to becoming the person your goals demand of you. Forget willpower. When properly designed, your systems do most of the heavy lifting for you. The systems within your business, whether people, technologies, or knowledge, can be intentionally harnessed for compounding effects. Personal habits, such as the five-hour rule, are systems that maximize your own insights and effort toward mastery. Good personal systems create the momentum to carry you forward with ease.

Benjamin Franklin was one to reinvent himself, embracing many careers throughout his life. Among his entrepreneurial achievements, Franklin invented the swim fins, the lightning rod, bifocal glasses, and the odometer. He did such meaningful work across disparate fields because he understood the power of personal systems.

Specifically, his systems helped him stay true and accountable to himself while defining and redefining how to serve others. Franklin's daily system included a morning reflection during which he set his intentions by asking "What good shall I do this day?" He divided his workday into blocks of time, each focused on the most meaningful and creative tasks. At the end of the day, Franklin evaluated what he had accomplished by asking himself, "What good have I done today?" He also frequently tracked his adherence to a set of 13 personal values, such as temperance, silence, and frugality, using a chart to mark his progress and areas for improvement. Together, these personal habits kept him focused on removing any blockers standing in the way of his potential. Though he developed his personal system in the 1700s, Franklin's routine is just as relevant today as a means to stay focused on one's highest point of personal leverage.

You have to figure out what leverage you can use, because there is always leverage, and if you find it, you'll do a lot better. —PAUL GRAHAM, Y COMBINATOR

From an inner perspective, your personal systems—your emotional and psychological patterns—guide your mind toward either lightness or darkness. Depending on your internal narrative, mental systems can either add or alleviate stress.

Anatomy of systems

Thinking in Systems by Donella Meadows is a fantastic introduction to the art and science of systems. Systems are everywhere: from traffic lights to pandemics to fashion trends to financial markets. At their essence, all systems consist of three things: inputs, output, and feedback loops.

Take the global human population as an example of a complex, adaptive system. First, the output of this system is the population count, 8.2 billion people at present. Secondly, the inputs are the rates of birth and death that influence population count over time. The global birth rate has been steadily going down since the 1950s, declining around one percent annually. The growth in death rate has been positive since 2019, rising around 0.5 percent annually. Knowing only this information, you can deduce that the global population is not rising as fast as it did in the past.

The feedback loop is the way the data is fed back into the system—in this case, how the population is measured, such as running a census every five years—and how that updated data leads to new directions. Based on the measurement of the data (feedback), a government might intervene to influence the birth or death rates of its citizens, actively steering the output of the system in a desired direction. China took such population-control measures with its one-child policy starting in 1979.

What China might not have considered initially with the population system is how their decisions would lead to a compounding change of inputs. In this case, this compounding effect worked in reverse, and China looks set for an unstoppable population decline. By 2100, China's population is expected to be 525 million people, a decrease of over 60 percent from its current 1.4 billion people. The original intention of the one-child policy was to control population growth and help modernize the Chinese economy, but the Chinese government did not understand the full ramification of single children having to potentially support two parents and four aging grandparents. The decline in birth rate from the one-child policy fed on itself from one generation to the next, with population growth falling further and further as decades went on.

By 2015, China came to realize that the policy was leading to an aging population much faster than anticipated, setting the table for a shrinking workforce, gender imbalances, and long-term economic challenges. A clearer understanding of population dynamics prompted the government to gradually relax the policy. As of 2021, Chinese parents are now allowed, even encouraged, to have three children. Still, the one-child policy will be felt for generations into the future. Complex and dynamic systems like demographics can be extremely powerful—so powerful that they become impossible to control.

Two categories of feedback loops

Like a game of snakes and ladders, the systems a founder encounters can help them compound the results (ladders) or move back (snakes). It's important to learn to spot the types of systems you encounter in the wild, so that you can position yourself accordingly.

First off, not all systems are equally helpful, and not all feedback loops behave the same way. The key is to recognize what you're dealing with: compounding or balancing systems. Those two systems behave differently. By understanding the anatomy of systems, you can then decide how to best engage with that system—or avoid getting stuck in it.

> *A bad system will beat a good person every time. This highlights the importance of focusing on systems design to create environments where individuals can succeed.*
> —W. EDWARDS DEMING

Compounding systems have a reinforcing feedback loop. Typically, their output grows over time. Population growth is a compounding system. Compounding systems also rule the growth of your business and the growth of your net worth. Compounding means momentum: The more you grow today, the easier future growth becomes. Compounding systems can also apply to intangible aspects of being a founder, like building your existing network and deepening your domain knowledge.

In contrast to compounding systems, *balancing systems* have self-reverting feedback loops—their output hovers around an output baseline. Deviating from the point of equilibrium will result in a natural course correction back toward the baseline. Let's say you have too much inventory compared to the current demand for your products. You adjust the system by reducing excess inventory levels, such as by doing a sale, and you return to a desired baseline. Inversely, if you notice that demand for a product is growing fast, you may order more products or increase the price to keep your inventory at the desired level.

Founders can't change the intrinsic nature of a system, just like they can't reorganize the natural order of things. The best thing a founder can do is clearly recognize what is unfolding in front of them, and work with—not against—that reality.

Systems thinking in entrepreneurship

As a founder, you need to harness one very important system: the collective expertise of your team. It is your responsibility as a leader to make sure that your people are well equipped to meet the challenges in front of them. You have a vested interest in shaping your team's know-how, through hiring the best people, training, promotions, and so on. People's specific knowledge and insight are subject to a compounding loop; for example, smart experts in a domain want to work with other smart experts because together they can generate better insights. Having a deep and varied expertise across your team makes it so much easier to further attract the best people who are willing to tackle the hard problems. That desire for advancing knowledge results in further collective insights. Here's a sample of compounding and balancing systems that founders are typically responsible for managing.

GOOD AND BAD
(ENTREPRENEURIAL) LOOPS

SYSTEMS	GOOD LOOPS	BAD LOOPS
Money	**Reinvesting Profits:** Increased cash flow leads to more reinvestment potential and growth.	**Accumulating Debt:** Interest on debt grows, consuming more revenue and reducing available capital for growth.
		Inflation: Rising costs reduce profit margins and purchasing power, making it harder to invest in growth opportunities.
Brand	**Building Brand and Customer Loyalty:** Positive customer experiences lead to repeat business and referrals, enhancing brand strength.	**Reputational Damage:** Negative events damage reputation, leading to loss of customers and reduced investor trust, which further harms the business.

Technology	**Technological Advancements:** Investments in technology lead to efficiency and scalability, which can be further invested in new technologies.	**Technological Debt:** Lack of appropriate response to technology trends results in loss of relevance and market share.

Short feedback loops are your friend

One thing is true for all systems: The shorter distance there is between action (input) and results (output) in a system, the better the decisions you can make. Observing cause and effect between input and output in real time makes it much easier to know how to adjust. With short feedback loops, your insights are more actionable. Short feedback loops are how you get to 10,000 iterations: Isolate a single input variable, test how it changes the output, adjust it, and continue iterating inputs endlessly with the next variable. Each iteration might be too small to amount to anything;

the real strength lies in the system that enables you to experiment quickly and cheaply. Over time, the speed of iteration is tied to the speed of feedback. To me, how fast a founder gathers feedback and iterates on it is the single best pattern predictor of entrepreneurial success.

> *If you can double the number of experiments you do per year, you're going to double your inventiveness. This concept of a feedback loop is crucial in business. The more you experiment and get feedback, the better you can refine your ideas and processes.* —PARAPHRASING JEFF BEZOS

Systems are not just about engineering. You can apply the same principles to your emotional systems.

If you water the seeds of anger in yourself, you will become angry more often. Same is true for love, joy, and hope.

By nurturing positive emotions intentionally (e.g., showing appreciation) and avoiding self-imposed suffering (e.g., getting into dumb arguments), you are harnessing the laws of inner systems. You can learn to intentionally compound positive emotions while balancing out the negative ones. This inner work is a lifelong journey, much like the path of Buddhist monks as they cultivate their minds toward enlightenment and the end of suffering.

THE TALE OF THE MONK AND THE TRAVELER

In a small village up in the mountains lived a wise monk. One day, a traveler arrived in the village, his heart heavy with resentment and his mind clouded with suffering. He had been wronged by a friend, and the seeds of anger within him had grown. Having heard of the monk's wisdom, the traveler sought him out, hoping to find justification and validation.

He found the monk tending to the garden outside the temple, carefully watering the plants. Approaching the monk, the traveler began to recount his tale of betrayal, expecting the monk to water his seeds of anger with words of agreement and commiseration. As the traveler spoke, however, the monk continued to water his garden in silence, his calm presence like a cool shade on a hot day.

After the traveler finished his story, the monk finally spoke. "See these plants in my garden? They grow strong and healthy because I water them daily and ensure they receive enough sunlight. There are also seeds of weeds among them, but I choose not to water those. If I did, they would overtake the garden, choking the life from these beautiful plants."

The traveler was puzzled. "But what does your garden have to do with my anger?"

"In every heart, there are seeds of anger, sadness, joy, and peace," the monk said. "Which seeds we choose to water determines the garden of our mind. If you water the seeds of anger, they will grow and suffocate your peace and happiness. But if you choose to water the seeds of forgiveness and understanding, your heart will be filled with peace and joy."*

> *Holding on to anger is like grasping a hot coal with the intent of throwing it at someone else; you are the one who gets burned.* —BUDDHAGHOṢA

---

* To explore this concept more deeply, I recommend watching the short video "Taking Care of Anger" by Thich Nhat Hanh: www.youtube.com/watch?v=9OvLOna5_1A.

The Hill You Will Gladly Die On

Life is not a problem to be solved,
but a reality to be experienced.
—SØREN KIERKEGAARD

Sooner or later, most founders encounter a life situation that feels so challenging, so painful, and so humbling that it brings them to a moment of surrender. As difficult as these moments can be, overwhelming struggle is a normal part of your hero's journey. With the benefit of age and experience, I've come to see more clearly that the way I embrace my lows is what ultimately defines my fate. So I embrace those lows by welcoming the difficult emotions too. Pain can be the ideal teacher, if you let it be. Surrendering is not the same as giving up.

Although painful mistakes in entrepreneurship are guaranteed, I believe that founders can save themselves some emotional struggle by understanding how the expectations they create influence their emotions.

Given that you've become good at solving problems for a living, you might be tempted to approach everything as a problem to be solved. I love solving problems, sometimes even when there are no problems to begin with. With only a hammer, everything starts looking like a nail. But life is ultimately more than hammering nails. Life is a voyage, not a puzzle. As crazy as it might sound, you don't have to fix anything. If you're seeing problems to solve everywhere, you might want to reevaluate how you form your expectations. Maybe that's where a lot of these troubles are coming from.

Expectations are beliefs and assumptions you hold about the future. On one hand, holding high expectations can be a self-fulfilling prophecy. Expecting excellent work might help your team rise to your high standards and achieve something they didn't know they had in them. On the other hand, low expectations can save you from the brutal sting of failure and disappointment. When should you have high or low expectations?

High vs. low expectations is another duality paradox. From my own experience, expectations should adjust based on the time horizon—the larger the time horizon, the larger the expectation. Finally, expect to be disappointed a portion of the time. That includes your expectations of yourself. Your expectations should leave a margin of error—we're all flawed, complex, and unpredictable humans.

Positive expectations or false hope?

James Stockdale was held captive for over seven years during the Vietnam War. He observed that the most optimistic prisoners often fared the worst, because they were crushed when their expectations were not met, having falsely expected, for example, that they would be released by Christmas Day. Stockdale maintained his will to survive by accepting the powerlessness of his reality while retaining faith that he would eventually prevail. This mindset, termed the "Stockdale Paradox," involves balancing unwavering faith in eventual success with the discipline to face a brutal reality.

This paradoxical mindset holds high and low expectations simultaneously: high expectations in the long term, low expectations in the short term. It's an attitude I've observed among outstanding founders too. They believe their success is inevitable, while expecting, even relishing, failures and adversity along the way. Managing your expectations effectively saves you emotional turmoil.

The fruit and the labor

Steve Jobs was famous for repeating the old adage "The journey is the reward." To me, the biggest factor in Jobs being one of history's most impactful founders was his ability to hold both extremely high and low expectations simultaneously. He chose his journey for the journey itself, with no expectation of outside success, motivated intrinsically to "make insanely great products," wherever that might take him, all while letting go of any expectations of specific results. Jobs held very high expectations in terms of the quality of design, but he focused on the act of creation itself. Today Jobs is remembered for his successful products, but we forget he shipped a bunch of failed product ideas: the Apple Lisa, NeXT Computer, Newton handheld, Macintosh TV, and iTunes Ping to name a few.

"The journey is the reward" is a timeless and universal mantra. The Bhagavad Gita, an ancient Hindu scripture written around 200–400 BCE, explores a crucial paradox that founders encounter to this day: how to pour yourself into your creative calling while detaching from expectations of results. According to the Gita, "You have a right to perform your prescribed duties, but you are not entitled to the fruits of your actions. Never consider yourself to be the cause of the results of your activities."*

Embracing this philosophy made Jobs bolder and more tolerant of failure. When he returned for his second stint at Apple in 1997, he was looking at failure dead in the eyes. The company was weeks away

---

* Bhagavad Gita, chapter 2, verse 47.

from bankruptcy. Without pressure to conform to high market expectations, Jobs could see clearly what Apple needed and went on to lead one of the most epic turnarounds ever. Unimpeded by fear, he felt more apt to make the concentrated, contrarian bets that gave us the iPod, iPhone, and iPad.

A fearless mind free from expecting results is a powerful combination: This is the mindset of someone with nothing to lose. Think about this: What would you keep doing *even if* failure was assured? If you are doing something hard and new, try starting with the assumption that failure is the likely scenario. Because it is. Assuming failure in this case is not pessimism; it gives you freedom to do your best work. If you can find true inner motivation to pursue your path regardless of success or failure, then nothing can stand in your way.

Choosing your "hill to die on" ultimately helps you clarify your deepest intentions. Defining and owning your symbolic hill creates a healthy distance between you and your expectations for the future. Find something you want to create so badly, something that needs to exist so much, that it makes all your sacrifices worthwhile in the end.

Paradoxically, when you don't expect results and don't buy into fear of failure, your labor might yield more "fruit" than you could ever get otherwise. What should you do when all these bounties come your way? Help others and further your sense of purpose. These fruits were not for you to expect nor hoard. Sharing the abundance in your life will only multiply your wealth.

The Buddha taught that generosity brings happiness at every stage of its expression. We experience joy in forming the intention to be generous. We experience joy in the actual act of giving something. We also experience joy in remembering the fact that we have given.

You have not lived today until you have done something for someone who can never repay you. —JOHN BUNYAN

Your Startup Is Not Your Identity

Your value doesn't decrease based on someone's inability to see your worth. —ZIG ZIGLAR

Behind the scenes, many founders struggle with a fragile identity. Entrepreneurs can become completely entangled in their work, so emotionally absorbed that they lose sight of other areas of their lives. Your startup should not become your entire identity. Fixating on one single role in your life as your main source of self-worth makes your identity so vulnerable to outside events that are out of your reach. Fixation makes you fragile.

I've been there. I'd feel good about myself only when my startup was going well, and I'd feel worthless when our company struggled. I felt only as good as my last battle, so I constantly needed fresh wins to justify my own worth. A minor mistake felt like hard evidence of my worthlessness. At a point in my life, fear of failure had me paralyzed.

Fearing failure every hour of the day leaves you in a place of emotional chaos. I'm sure you've felt it too. Perhaps you lost sleep over a comment one customer made, or maybe you agonized over the time it takes to ship a new feature. I get it—it's scary to work for years toward your life's purpose and have nothing to show for it yet. The idea of going down a dead-end road for years is painful to imagine for any founder.

As part of my founder journey, I hit an emotional bottom in the months after selling our company, which I want to stress was an overall positive event for my team and me. I'll forever be grateful to Shopify leaders for seeing the potential in us. Shopify truly was the ideal place for me to work on bettering myself at that point in my life. But as a new employee integrating into a large organization, I felt pressured to live up to my identity: a startup superhero. I felt the necessity to not disappoint myself or others, no matter what. I'd had some success, only to feel even more terrified of failure.

A lifetime of seeking external approval as permission to feel good about myself was catching up to me. I realized I had become overly focused on not losing instead of winning. I didn't want to disappoint anyone. The traditional signs of success were present in my life, yet I still couldn't think of myself as a good, worthy person. It was all about my shortcomings. *Don't fail, no matter what*, I'd repeat to myself. I couldn't congratulate myself for anything positive. The cracks in my expiring identity were starting to show. I was depressed. I was unmotivated. I didn't recognize my "normal" self. That's when I truly began the inner work as a founder.

As mentally challenging as this episode was, I'm glad it drove me to understand how my inner and outer realities had become disconnected. My inner monologue was faulty, gripped by fear of failure. My self-esteem was riding on one single dimension of my life. My life felt binary, black and white, win or lose, with nothing in between. I was trapped in duality.

The emotional pain drove me to find and fix the faulty beliefs that impaired my self-narrative, with the help of a coach and a therapist. I am so grateful I met many brilliant founders and builders in my years at Shopify that led me to entirely rethink how I approach "success" and "failure." As a result, I now feel more at ease with the volatile path that entrepreneurship is— good, bad, and ugly.

Mind the expectations you place on yourself

Founders generally believe they are smart and talented. They have to. Having confidence in your own potential goes a very long way when your livelihood depends on being right, seeing around corners, and making high-stakes decisions. Naturally, founders place high expectations on themselves, sometimes trying to become nothing short of a superhero. That's because they are instinctively aware of their potential, and their work happens to be the vessel that propels them toward their destiny.

That said, the higher the expectations you place on yourself, the harder it becomes to experience satisfaction in who you are at this moment. Imagine you are building a Jenga tower: the higher you stack expectations, the more unstable your identity becomes as a whole. As you keep adding to the tower, it becomes harder to reach the expectations you created for yourself. Your self-image gets shaky, eventually something upsets you, and your identity tips over. Suffering ensues.

A healthy self-image means believing you can figure it out

> *Self-esteem is the reputation we acquire with ourselves.* —NATHANIEL BRANDEN, AUTHOR OF *SIX PILLARS OF SELF-ESTEEM*

How to form a solid, healthy self-image? First, by not commanding yourself to be a superhero, and by adopting realistic expectations for yourself. I believe a healthy self-image doesn't require you to perform at the highest level of excellence. A healthy self-image means believing you can figure *this* out, welcoming setbacks and failures to help you learn, given enough time and effort.

Forming an identity distinct from your entrepreneurial pursuits can be tricky when you're emotionally, physically, intellectually, and financially all in. The thing is, for your dreams to come true, you have to sell other people on your dream. And when you're convincing others to buy into your story, it does help to be seen as a winner. Confidence in the face of hardships is contagious. That's why entrepreneurship is largely a confidence game.

"Confidence precedes competence" is a mantra I often hear among founders. History is full of founders, creators, and innovators who took on challenges they were clearly not equipped to face at that time, while also believing with total certainty in their potential and their ability to rise to the occasion. We've seen how James Cameron takes on hard movies. Each of his biggest hits was a masterpiece from a visual technology standpoint. Without confidence, Cameron and his team wouldn't have persisted in the face of technically impossible projects.

Still, I've often wondered if self-confidence is just something you're born with, like a genetic winning lottery ticket. Modern entrepreneurial heroes can exude extreme levels of confidence, bordering on delusion. Watching Elon Musk explain with a straight face how SpaceX is going to Mars in our lifetime, it's easy to think he was born with it. Maybe there is a place in history for the grandiose egos like Musk or Napoleon, but that said, history also has a place for great founders who became confident over time, as they gained competence. Among them are Katharine Graham and Christian Dior, both of whom gradually overcame their self-doubt, building confidence one challenge at a time. They show that self-confidence is mostly a skill.

For example, Katharine Graham inherited the roles of publisher and majority owner at the *Washington Post* in 1963, after her husband sadly died by suicide. Born into a rich family and having spent her entire adult life in the supportive roles of wife and mother, she had not been prepared for a leadership position. Graham initially lacked confidence due to traditional gender roles and her sudden new responsibilities after her husband's death. Writing in her memoir, *Personal History*, she says:

I was always uncomfortable, always questioning myself and my decisions. I constantly worried that I wasn't up to the task, that I would fail and let everyone down. I was acutely aware of the skepticism around me. Many people, both inside and outside the company, doubted my ability to lead. It took years of hard work and many difficult decisions before I began to feel confident in my role.[*]

Ultimately Graham became a highly effective leader and respected by employees, customers, and investors. If you'd invested in the *Washington Post* in 1971 when it went public, your stake would have been 89 times larger by the time Graham stepped down in 1993—a return 6 times larger than her industry peers, and 18 times larger than the S&P 500 over the same period.

Similarly, Christian Dior did not innately believe he could become a fashion icon. He had severe self-doubt before starting his own label. He even walked away briefly just before the brand launched, despite being

---

[*] Graham, *Personal History*, 135.

served the opportunity of a lifetime on a silver platter. Dior was unsure of himself but went ahead anyway. He had to build confidence on the job. A year after launch, his fashion house hit gold with the "New Look" collection. Although Dior became a known brand, behind the scenes, Christian was still feeling intense anxiety and self-doubt. His chronic worries about not being good enough drove him to define effective coping strategies: assemble a highly trusted team, demand excellent workmanship, and pour passion into the products. Dior coped by trusting in his creative process when he didn't trust himself. He pushed back on his anxiety by adopting the confident persona of "Christian Dior, the Designer," which exuded certainty and decisiveness. This alter ego helped him channel his energies and project confidence. He gradually became more comfortable and confident leading his company. Dior is still an enduring brand 80 years later.

My point is that Graham and Dior didn't seem like obvious entrepreneurs; they grappled with self-doubt—and that's okay. What they always held was the belief that they had potential, that they could *figure things out*. So they did.

Confidence grows with good mental habits

If self-confidence is a skill, then it can be trained. I've relied on a few techniques to actively build confidence. Maybe they can help you too.

Choose each word with care. Specific words shape your internal narrative, and that narrative shapes how you feel about yourself. Each word matters. Negative self-talk is a form of self-sabotage: A destructive narrative might stop you from trying in the first place. Choose precise words that support the most empowering version of your narrative.

Zoom out. To understand how far you've come, take a view of the trajectory of your entire journey. Where did it start? Where are you heading? By zooming out to see your entire founder story, it's easier to see that you are not your last win or loss. Zooming out makes it clear that patience is a virtue and time is our ally.

Believe your potential is infinite. Anchor your confidence in your innately human potential to learn and grow. There is no ceiling on your potential. An identity built on resilience and the resolve to figure things out along the way injects a sense of adventure and curiosity even in dire and draining situations.

Designing identity for resilience

Once you agree that you as a founder are more than your startup, your identity starts to feel more malleable. By being rooted in healthy expectations, it is not at risk of collapse. To be more resilient, make your identity small, broad, and imperfectly unique.

MAKE YOUR IDENTITY SMALL

Keeping your identity small means avoiding strong beliefs about who you are and how things should be in your life.* A smaller identity doesn't require as much energy to protect your ego. A small house is less work to maintain than a large one. Minimizing your identity gets you freedom. A small identity means there is less

---

* See Paul Graham's post "Keep Your Identity Small": https://paulgraham.com/identity.html.

to be offended about; you take things less personally. As an identity minimalist, unattached to any solid definition of who you are, you can interact with the world with clarity and humility.

MAKE YOUR IDENTITY BROAD

Broadening your identity means defining yourself through multiple dimensions, by forming a series of distinct stories about who you are and who you want to become. You are not dependent on a single narrative that could wreck your self-worth if it is threatened. You are a founder, but maybe you are also—and equally—a spouse, a parent, a friend, an athlete, a musician. Nurturing a portfolio of identities will bring you a stronger and more resilient sense of self.[*] Paradoxically, you might also become a better founder than if you had put all your identity eggs in a single entrepreneurial basket. When your startup struggles, the other roles in your life can help you stay emotionally afloat, providing the energy needed to weather adversity and change.

---

[*] See *Master of Change: How to Excel When Everything Is Changing—Including You* by Brad Stulberg for more about nurturing a portfolio of identities.

MAKE YOUR IDENTITY
IMPERFECTLY UNIQUE

Kintsugi is a traditional Japanese art form of repairing broken pottery using lacquer mixed with powdered gold. The result is stunning. The philosophy behind kintsugi is to embrace, even elevate, flaws and imperfections. A broken piece can be put back together, with beautiful, unique scars, and become a work of art. Let your defects shine through, let them define you, celebrate them as part of your identity. We all have something unique, something weird about ourselves. Learning to love your imperfections gives you the confidence to show up exactly as you are.

> *The Master stays behind; that is why she is ahead. She is detached from all things; that is why she is one with them. Because she has let go of herself, she is perfectly fulfilled.*
> —LAO TZU

Your Worth Comes from Trying, Not Winning

As Kevin Kelly puts it, "Many fail to finish, but many more fail to start. The hardest work in any work is to start. You can't finish until you start, so get good at starting."[*] I suspect the main reason that people fail to take their first step is because they fear failure. But the fact that you're trying when others don't even try is itself

---

[*] See Kevin Kelly's post "101 Additional Advices" in his online series The Technium: https://kk.org/thetechnium/101-additional -advices/.

immensely valuable. That first step is the most valuable, because it is the step that sets you on a new trajectory.

Your destiny as a founder is to grow into your own potential, to tell your own hero's journey. Only by freeing yourself of your dysfunctional emotional patterns, and by working honestly on becoming a better person in the face of adversity, uncertainty, stress, and doubt, can you reach your ultimate destiny.

In his book *How Innovation Works: And Why It Flourishes in Freedom*, Matt Ridley outlines how entrepreneurial collaboration and failure are the very fabric of innovation. He makes the point that individual failure is an essential component of innovation. Willingness to iterate in the face of failure is critical for progress, as each individual failure provides valuable learning experiences that pave the way for future successes, just as the new generation of founders build on the work of their predecessors. In aggregate, entrepreneurship operates inside a giant system of innovation built on the cumulative and collective knowledge gained through many individual pursuits over time. We are part of a never-ending iterative process of collective learning and adaptation going back to the beginning of human history.

Famously, many entrepreneurs worked on giving us the lightbulb we know today. Although Thomas Edison is credited for making this innovation mainstream, he was only standing on the shoulders of other founders, learning from their failed past attempts. Edison recombined existing insights in a new way, as opposed to having a "lightbulb moment." Edison did not invent electrical lighting by himself; his contribution was to make the technology commercially viable and accessible to all. Today we use electricity thanks to countless failed attempts by long-forgotten innovators, more so than because of a single breakthrough by a single man.

Your worth comes from the very act of entrepreneurship, from taking that first step. And then the next one. Your value lies in your motion, not your results. The individual failures of entrepreneurs are what bring us all forward collectively.

Nassim Taleb makes that same point In *Antifragile: Things That Gain from Disorder*:

In order to progress, modern society should be treating ruined entrepreneurs in the same way we honor dead soldiers, perhaps not with as much honor, but using exactly the same logic (the entrepreneur is still alive, though perhaps morally broken and socially stigmatized, particularly if he lives in Japan). For there is no such thing as a failed soldier, dead or alive (unless he acted in a cowardly manner)—likewise, there is no such thing as a failed entrepreneur or failed scientific researcher.*

I end this book on the topic of failure not to discourage you, but to free you to embrace your own founder journey. Take that first step even if you're scared. Fear of failure is only a burden if it keeps you from taking that step. Deciding to go after your dreams in spite of your fears and doubts is the right way to live, to make the most of your time in this life. Living with courage is to live freely. You are free to define your own success, your own values, your own story. Remember, most people don't even start. Precisely where your business ends up isn't as important where your founder journey takes you.

---

* Taleb, *Antifragile*, 112.

Entrepreneurs are heroes in our society. They fail for the rest of us.

—NASSIM TALEB

BIBLIOGRAPHY

Averett, Nancy. "I'm a Runner: Sir James Dyson." *Runner's World*, August 1, 2009. www.runnersworld.com/runners-stories /a20837443/im-a-runner-sir-james-dyson/.

The Bhagavad Gita. Translated by Eknath Easwaran. Tomales, CA: Nilgiri, 2007.

Bezos, Jeff. "2015 Letter to Shareholders." ir.aboutamazon.com, Annual reports, proxies and shareholder letters, April 2016. https://s2.q4cdn.com/299287126/files/doc_financials/annual /2015-Letter-to-Shareholders.PDF.

Bezos, Jeff. "2017 Letter to Shareholders." ir.aboutamazon.com, Annual reports, proxies and shareholder letters, April 2018. https://s2.q4cdn.com/299287126/files/doc_financials/annual /Amazon_Shareholder_Letter.pdf.

Brach, Tara. "Disarming Our Hearts: Guidance from the Bodhisattva Path, Part 1." Lecture, June 5, 2024. www.youtube.com /watch?v=iG03XwxXM-k.

Branden, Nathaniel. *Six Pillars of Self-Esteem*. New York: Bantam Books, 1994.

Burkeman, Oliver. *Four Thousand Weeks: Time Management for Mortals*. New York: Farrar, Straus and Giroux, 2021.

Catmull, Ed, and Amy Wallace. *Creativity, Inc.: Overcoming the Unseen Forces That Stand in the Way of True Inspiration.* New York: Random House, 2014.

Christensen, Clayton. *How Will You Measure Your Life?* New York: Harper Business, 2012.

Clear, James. *Atomic Habits.* New York: Avery, 2018.

Covey, Stephen, A. Roger Merrill, and Rebecca R. Merrill. *First Things First.* New York: Free Press, 1994.

De Dreu, C. K. W., and L. R Weingart. "Task Versus Relationship Conflict, Team Performance, and Team Member Satisfaction: A Meta-analysis." *Journal of Applied Psychology* 88, no. 4 (2003): 741-749. DOI: 10.1037/0021-9010.88.4.741.

Dyson, James. *Against the Odds.* Orion, 1997.

Ericsson, K. Anders, Ralf Th. Krampe, and Clemens Tesch-Romer. "The Role of Deliberate Practice in the Acquisition of Expert Performance." *Psychological Review* 100, no. 3 (1993): 363–406.

Farnam Street. "Create and Curate." Farnam Street Brain Food blog, July 2, 2023. https://fs.blog/brain-food/july-2-2023/.

Gladwell, Malcolm. *Outliers: The Story of Success.* New York: Little, Brown and Company, 2008.

Graham, Katharine. *Personal History.* New York: Vintage Books, 1998.

Graham, Paul. www.paulgraham.com/articles.html.

Haden, Jeff. "The Fundamental Difference Between Decisions and Actions: Why Jeff Bezos Says Your Goal Is to Make 3 Good Decisions per Day." *Inc.*, November 3, 2022, www.inc.com

/jeff-haden/jeff-bezos-difference-between-decisions-actions-make-3-good-decisions-per-day.html.

Hanh, Thich Nhat. *Taming the Tiger Within: Meditations on Transforming Difficult Emotions.* New York: Riverhead Books, 2004.

Hanh, Thich Nhat. *The Heart of the Buddha's Teaching: Transforming Suffering into Peace, Joy, and Liberation.* New York: Broadway Books, 1999.

Holiday, Ryan. *Ego Is the Enemy.* New York: Portfolio, 2016.

Horowitz, Ben. *The Hard Thing About Hard Things: Building a Business When There Are No Easy Answers.* New York: Harper Business, 2014.

Isaacson, Walter. *Steve Jobs.* New York: Simon & Schuster, 2011.

Jorgenson, Eric. *The Almanack of Naval Ravikant: A Guide to Wealth and Happiness.* Lexington, KY: Magrathea Publishing, 2020.

Kelly, Kevin. *Excellent Advice for Living: Wisdom I Wish I'd Known Earlier.* New York: Viking, 2023.

LaFreniere, Lucas S., and Michelle G. Newman. "Exposing Worry's Deceit: Percentage of Untrue Worries in Generalized Anxiety Disorder Treatment." *Behavior Therapy* 51, no. 3 (2020): 413–23. https://doi.org/10.1016/j.beth.2019.07.003.

Lansing, Alfred. *Endurance: Shackleton's Incredible Voyage.* New York: Basic Books, 1959.

Lao Tzu. Tao Te Ching. Translated by Stephen Mitchell. New York: Harper & Row, 1988.

Lee, Shannon. *Be Water, My Friend: The Teachings of Bruce Lee.* New York: Flatiron Books, 2020.

Macrotrends. "World Birth Rate 1950-2024." *Macrotrends*. Accessed October 15, 2024. https://www.macrotrends.net /global-metrics/countries/WLD/world/birth-rate.

Macrotrends. "World Death Rate 1950-2024." *Macrotrends*. Accessed October 15, 2024. https://www.macrotrends.net /global-metrics/countries/WLD/world/death-rate.

Manjoo, Farhad. "Snap Makes a Bet on the Cultural Supremacy of the Camera." New York Times, March 8, 2017. www.nytimes .com/2017/03/08/technology/snap-makes-a-bet-on-the-cultural-supremacy-of-the-camera.html.

Manson, Mark. *The Subtle Art of Not Giving a F*ck: A Counterintuitive Approach to Living a Good Life*. New York: HarperOne, 2016.

Matthews, John, and Matthew McKay. *Self-Esteem: A Proven Program of Cognitive Techniques for Assessing, Improving, and Maintaining Your Self-Esteem*. Narrated by Patrick Fanning. Audiobook. Audible, 2016.

McKeown, Greg. *Essentialism: The Disciplined Pursuit of Less*. New York: Crown, 2020.

Meadows, Donella. *Thinking in Systems: A Primer*. White River Junction, VT: Chelsea Green, 2008.

Packard, David. *The HP Way: How Bill Hewlitt and I Built Our Company*. New York: Harper Collins, 2013.

Parrish, Shane. *The Great Mental Models: General Thinking Concepts*. Farnam Street Media, 2019.

Pressfield, Steven. *The War of Art: Break Through the Blocks and Win Your Inner Creative Battles*. New York: Black Irish Entertainment, 2002.

Rubin, Rick. *The Creative Act: A Way of Being*. New York: Penguin, 2023.

Ridley, Matt. *How Innovation Works: And Why It Flourishes in Freedom*. New York: Harper, 2020.

Singer, Michael A. *The Untethered Soul: The Journey Beyond Yourself*. Oakland, CA: New Harbinger, 2007.

Sivers, Derek. *Hell Yeah or No: What's Worth Doing*. United States: Hit Media, 2022.

Stulberg, Brad. *Master of Change: How to Excel When Everything Is Changing—Including You*. New York: HarperOne, 2023.

Taleb, Nassim Nicholas. *Antifragile: Things That Gain from Disorder*. New York: Random House, 2012.

Thorndike, William N. *The Outsiders: Eight Unconventional CEOs and Their Radically Rational Blueprint for Success*. Boston: Harvard Business Review Press, 2012.

Van Doren, Paul. *Authentic: A Memoir*. New York: William Morrow, 2021.

Ware, Bronnie. *The Top Five Regrets of the Dying: A Life Transformed by the Dearly Departing*. Carlsbad, CA: Hay House, 2012.

ABOUT THE AUTHOR

Guillaume Racine is a Canadian entrepreneur and investor. His early ventures as a musician chasing artistic dreams led him to pursue a creative path in life, specifically through the craft of entrepreneurship. With an MBA from INSEAD and a bachelor's degree from HEC Montreal, he was previously co-founder and CEO at Return Magic, a startup acquired by Shopify. Nowadays he spends his time as a builder and investor in early-stage companies in software and commerce. Drawing from personal experiences, Guillaume shares timeless insights on the inner game of entrepreneurship in his first book *Tao of Founders*, hoping that he can help other founders on their journey too.

www.ingramcontent.com/pod-product-compliance
Lightning Source LLC
Chambersburg PA
CBHW020255130626
46549CB00005B/2229